Anna W. Ford Piper

Peak's Island

A Romance of Buccaneer Days

Anna W. Ford Piper

Peak's Island
A Romance of Buccaneer Days

ISBN/EAN: 9783744673594

Printed in Europe, USA, Canada, Australia, Japan

Cover: Foto ©Thomas Meinert / pixelio.de

More available books at **www.hansebooks.com**

CHAPTER I.

Roll on thou deep and dark blue ocean roll;
. . . . . . Upon the watery plain.
The wrecks are all thy deed, nor doth remain
A shadow of man's ravage, save his own,
When for a moment like a drop of rain,
He sinks into thy depths with bubbling groan,
Without a grave, unknelled, uncoffined, and unknown.

SEPTEMBER 27, 1607.

DEAD bodies everywhere. The ocean, lashed to fury by the gale of yesterday, came booming and hissing upon the beach in great breakers white with foam ; each billow as it dashed upon the jagged and broken rocks bore in its terrible embrace still more human victims, or some portion of the two unlucky ships that were fast breaking up. One wedged in between two rocks with just sufficient play to allow of its heaving from side to side, with every wave that struck it. The other and much larger vessel, the Queen Elizabeth, a fine British ship, which had sailed from England freighted with a cargo of general merchandise for the colony of Virginia, went crashing up against the cruel stone teeth of the cliff which overhung and projected into the angry sea; dismasted, her bulwarks and rigging torn away she floated out into deeper water only to be driven back again upon the rocks, by the violence of the wind and the rapidly incoming tide.

Another crash and another, the forecastle carried away, the decks opening, bales, chests, cor-
dage, stores of all sorts tossed high up on the
shore, more dead bodies—chiefly of men, for they
had some time before given up to the few women
and children the now capsized and shattered boats.
All along the shore, as far as eye could see, the
beach was composed of a heterogeneous mass of
enormous fragments of rock thrown together and
piled up on each other, leaving here and there in
their midst a separate pool of sea water ; in some
of these pools was a dead body or two, but by far
the greater number were lying in every imaginable,
distorted position among the huge, irregular blocks
of stone. Many, who had been washed in suffic-
iently far to escape drowning, were killed by the
force with which they were dashed on shore : there,
with broken bones and gnashed and blood-stained
bodies, they slept in death, like men who had fall-
en in some great battle. It was noon, but not a
ray of sunlight glinted across the ghastly scene.
Every sound was lost in the terrific roar of the
great, heaving hills of water, which rolled in con-
tinuously ; huge masses of wet gray cloud hung
over all, obscuring or transforming every visible object. Far up among the shingle lay one human
form which still bore signs of life. It was that of
a young lady, attired in deep mourning, a stream
of blood trickled down the pale face, and from time
to time one hand moved convulsively toward a
deep cut in her head as if to assuage the pain; presently in half-consciousness she whispered " Do not

tell my mother I am hurt, it would grieve her. She has had too much sorrow already."

The beloved mother, and all others who had made life precious to the speaker, had three years previously been tenderly laid to rest in their quiet graves thousands of miles away; but at this moment the mind had only half awakened. A few minutes later her brain was clear and active, and the truth flashed upon her in all its force. The recollection of her bereavement and the fact of her being utterly alone in life, were the first thoughts that came and the thoughts which dominated. And so it is that all who are called upon to endure a great sorrow, acutely realize that sorrow again and again with each return of the mind to the consciousness of human existence, whether it be after the delerium of fever, the stunning from an accident, or the awaking each morning to daily life. With the awaking to our senses assurely comes the old heartache; nay, before we awake it is there, and before we are conscious of aught else we are conscious of the grief which weighs heaviest on our soul. Thus it was with Anna Vyvyan: the awaking to life brought with it the pain in all its intensity, although she lay there on the cold stones, her clothing drenched through and through, bareheaded, her hair matted together with the sea water, bruised and cut and faint from exhaustion, still the present physical suffering seemed by comparison nothing to her. Everything was buried in the sorrow of the past, the sorrow that she had lived through, but had not left behind.

CHAPTER II.

The stately-homes of England
  How beautiful they stand,
Amidst their tall ancestral trees,
  O'er all the pleasant land!
The deer across their greensward bound
  Through shade and sunny gleam,
And the swan glides past them with the sound
  Of some rejoicing stream.

The merry homes of England —
  Around their hearths by night,
What gladsome looks of household love
  Meet in the ruddy light!
There women's voice flows forth in song
  Or childhood's tale is told
Or lips move tunefully along
  Some glorious page of old.

The blessed homes of England,
  How softly on their bowers,
Is laid the holy quietness
  That breathes from Sabbath hours
Solemn, yet sweet, the church bell's chime
  Floats through their woods at morn,
All other sounds at that still time
  Of breeze and leaf are born.

MISS VIVYAN was the daughter of an officer of high rank in the navy of Queen Elizabeth, who lost his life in the royal service while his little girl Anna was still very young. His valor had gained for him many medals and yet more substantial honors in the form of valuable grants of land from Her Majesty. This property, added to the family inheritance of Anna's mother, who was a lady of old and noble race, left both the widow and her child in very affluent circumstances. The young widow, handsome and possessed of brilliant talents, attracted many suitors for her hand; but her heart lay far down beneath the sea with her dead husband, and she resolved to devote her love and her life to the care of her child. She accordingly retired to an old manor house on the borders of Wales, which had descended to her through many generations. The great stone halls and corridors, the long, low rooms and the little diamond-shaped window panes, admitting so small an amount of light, might have given to some minds a feeling of gloom ; but both mother and daughter had their occupations, the one in giving, the other in receiving, an education, beside the care of all the sick and poor peasants of the neighborhood. Indeed they were so happy in their affection for each other and found so much to do, that they had neither the time nor the inclination to cultivate morbid or gloomy thoughts, which would, they felt, make their companionship an infliction on every one whom they approached, and unfit them for the duties of their position. So life went on calmly and happily with them.

A faithful steward attended to the estates and a good old housekeeper managed the servants, always keeping order, discipline and peace in the establishment. Twice a year they were allowed to have a dance in the servants' hall, one at Christmas and the other on Anna's birthday, on which occasions they invited the sons and daughters of the neighboring farmers, and the tradespeople who supplied the manor house. The village shoemaker, the tailor, and the blacksmith were the musicians, and to the strains of two violins and a clarionet, they merrily danced through the livelong night, such good old figures as Sir Roger de Coverly, Speed the Plough, and the Cushion dance, till the rising sun streamed in at the windows and warned them that it was time to blow out the candles, take off their holiday garb, and assume their daily work. As for the mistress of the mansion, she found her pleasures in the duties of her position and the rich companionship of a well stocked library. She had no neighbors of her own rank within several miles distance, no one to visit or to be visited by, with the exception of the old bachelor clergyman of the parish, whose formal calls took place at stated intervals, unless some sudden case of want among the poor caused him to ask her aid, for he knew very well that her heart and hand went forth on every occasion of distress. Hers it was to soothe and cheer and comfort and help, and many a thorny path was made smooth and many a heavy burden lifted by her brave and generous spirit and the pleasant, cheerful way she had of doing such things. In the presence of others she made a duty of cultivating cheerfulness of manner. Not that she ever for a moment forgot the recollection of her love and her loss; but she considered her sorrows too sacred for a subject of conversation on one hand, and on the other, that her grief was her own, and that she had no right to intrude it upon others, or to weigh down and sadden their lives by what was sent for her to bear. Hence her presence was always welcome to the peasants, who regarded her with reverence and affection, as she passed, accompanied by her little daughter, from cottage to cottage leaving some dainty for the sick, or an article of clothing for the needy.

Years went by and Anna had left babyhood far behind her and was now a girl of fifteen. Her mother at this period, decided that it was time to call in the aid of masters to assist in her daughter's education. Accordingly, such were summoned from a distant town. There was a master for the minuette and the gavotte, a master for the harpsichord, a master for the French and Italian lan. guages, and so on. The days and hours were all laid out systematically, giving an abundance of time for physical training and out-door life, but with the exception of the masters for music and dancing (more especially the former) none of these instructors made much impression upon the girl's mind. Her heart and soul were given to music While she was in the house her time was spent between the old church organ that stood in the hall, and the harpsicord which adorned the long, oak-panelled drawing-room. When out of doors she was forever listening to the music of nature, the wind through the trees, the dash of the water. fall, the rippling of the brook, all had their charm and fascination, for nature never played out of tune. She would try to make out what key these

sounds were in, whether they varied at different
seasons, or if change in the weather made them
alter,

Music was her passion, her love, her life.

Just at that time, two new inmates were added
to the manor house family. Young Cecil Vyvyan,
a cousin of Anna's, who was of the same age as
herself, and his tutor, Dr. Strickland, a grave, mid-
dle-aged Scotch doctor of philosophy. The boy's
parents were in India, which caused the widow to
suggest to them that he should, for a few years,
make his home with her, in order that she might
watch over his health, which was exceedingly delicate.

It was in the twilight of a day late in the autumn that Anna waited in the large old-fashioned
library to make the first acquaintance of her
cousin. In the broad stone fireplace, logs of beech
and chestnut were piled up on the hearth, across
brass dogs, where they blazed, and glowed, and
lighted up the comfortable looking room, with its
dark, massive, carved oak furniture, its painted
glass windows, its rich but faded velvet draperies,
interspersed here and there with a piece of old tapestry, the needlework of the ladies of former generations. A few family portraits, and well-filled
bookcases of vellum-bound octavos, quartos and
folios. As the butler threw open the door of the
room and announced Master Cecil Vyvyan, Anna
went forward to greet the latter, and almost gave a
start of surprise at seeing the real cousin differ so
much from the ideal one which she had pictured to

herself; for she expected to find Cecil of the same
type as the English boys that she had always seen.
She thought he would be large of his age, with a
fresh rosy complexion, bright eyes, an open coun-
tenance, crowned with masses of rich, curling
locks. Strong and healthy, overflowing with buoy-
ant spirits, agile and ready for active service either
of work or play. Instead of which there stood before her one of small stature and thin, diminutive
figure, with a pale, weary-looking face and tired
eyes, which apparently did not observe any of the
objects by which he was surrounded, but concentrated their gaze upon the young girl only, with
whom he stood face to face, carefully regarding her
with that scrutiny which we are all wont to use
when we first make the acquaintance of a new rel-
ative.

Anna gave him her hand and welcomed .him
with a few kind .words. As the boy and girl stood
there, no two cousins could have appeared more
.externally unlike, and yet never were two more
alike in their highest tastes and deepest feelings.
But an ordinary looker-on would only see the boy
so small, and quiet, and weary, and the girl so tall,
and active, and healthy, abounding in lively spirits,
in the full enjoyment of her young life, with the
mother she adored, thinking nothing could be more
beautiful than her picturesque old home and its
surroundings of hill and valley, and woodland, and
broad green meadows, and turning over in her
mind how she would show Cecil all the favorite
huants. The lily pond in the park, the finest view

of the Welsh mountains, and the right place for a good gallop — then the ponies, and the dogs, and the fish pools.

"You must be tired from so long a journey, Cousin Cecil," said she, "let me bring this arm-chair ; it is the most restful one in the whole house. It has a pedigree, too, the same as you and I have. It belonged to our great-grandfather, Sir Vyell Vyvyan, and was made more than a hundred years ago from one of the oaks which grew in the north grove in the park," so saying she laid one hand on the back of a huge, cumbersome piece of furniture, and rolled it across the room up in front of the glowing logs.

It was now Cecil's turn to be amazed, how could she move that great, clumsy thing, he pondered to himself, I could not. With a gentle thank you, and bowing gracefully to her, he sank into their great-grandfather's chair, and was almost lost sight of among the ample velvet cushions.

Anna who had seated herself on one side of the fireplace, was watching the pale face, and the weary eyes that were looking dreamily at the fantastic shapes which from time to time the glowing embers assumed. Presently a slight, convulsive shudder passed through the boy's frame and a quiet little sigh escaped him.

He is sad, thought Anna, perhaps he is thinking of his home in Calcutta, poor fellow, I must do something to amuse him. At the same instant, what she considered a very happy thought suggested itself.

"I am so glad you came, Cousin Cecil," said she "they say you will soon get well and strong here. I have a little terrier that catches rats, you shall take him out in the morning, if you like, and the gardener's boy will show you where you can kill plenty."

"I don't kill rats," he replied, still keeping his eyes fixed upon the burning logs and striving to follow the outlines of a fairy island with palms and tropical plants and ferns as tall as forest trees, which, in his imagination, he saw there.

"Do you go with your terrier to kill rats?" he inquired, with the slightest tone of sarcasm in his voice.

"Oh, no," replied the girl, "but I thought you would like to. Most boys are amused by it, they call it sport, and you know the rats must be killed or we should have them running behind the wainscot of all the rooms in the house, and the gamekeeper would not be able to rear the young pheasants, and we should have no chickens nor pigeons, nor anything of the kind."

"Why, Cousin Anna," said the boy, "have you a Scotch governess, and does she make you give a reason for every thing, and give you her reason in return? That's what Dr. Strickland does with me. It tires me dreadfully, and I don't see what use it is, for I always know things without reasoning about them; they come to me of themselves."

Anna, in her eagerness to show kindness to the guest of the house, and to divert what seemed to her his sad thoughts, did not stop to make any reply, but rose and hastily crossed over to one of the bookcases, bringing back in her arms a large folio, full of colored illustrations of field sports.

"Now, Cousin Cecil," said she, drawing up a chair close by the side of his, and laying the folio open upon her lap, "this will please you I am sure; this is not about rats, but thorough-bred horses and dogs, stag-hounds and fox-hounds. Did you ever hear that our grandfather kept a pack of fox-hounds here, that is a hundred dogs you know. I will take you to the kennels and the huntman's lodge some day soon." ·

Cecil did not know that a hundred dogs made a pack, for he had passed all his life in India, until a few months previous to his coming to the manor house.

"Look at this picture of coursing, here is another of hawking, and now see these otter hounds."

"The landscape is beautiful," said the boy. "I like the soft gray light on those distant hills in the background, but I do not care about pictures of horses and dogs ; please take them away. I like to see the animals moving in the fields, but I think all this kind of sport is very cruel."

This was said in an extremely gentle way, and at the same time with an inflection of the voice which made a deep impression upon his listener. I wonder what I can do to amuse him, thought Anna ; I don't suppose he would care to look at my last piece of embroidery, or hear how many sonatas I can play ; I am afraid he is sorry he came here, perhaps he was thinking of the Himalaya mountains, when he said he liked those hills in the picture. Most boys like out-door amusements, she again thought to herself, and acting upon the idea of the moment,

"Cecil," said she, "we have two capital ponies, we will go out in the forenoon to-morrow if you like, for we are to have a holiday from our studies all day, in honor of your coming here."

Again a gentle "thank you" from Cecil, his tired eyes still seeking air castles among the red and gray embers of the fire. After some minutes silence, he turned to look at the tall old clock in the corner, which, in addition to the hours and minutes depicted upon its face, was adorned with supposed likenesses of the sun and moon and other heavenly bodies, beside the terrestrial globe which represented Jerusalem as being situated in the very center of the earth's surface.

The same old clock, which had stood in the same corner of the library long enough to mark the hours of the births and marriages, the meetings and partings, and death, of several generations of the Vyvyans, now chimed in slow, subdued tones, through which ran the echo of a wail, like the voice of a human being, who has seen much and suffered much.

"Dr. Strickland will expect me to return to him now, Cousin Anna, so I must say "good evening.""

"Before you go, Cecil, tell me at what time you will be ready to ride with me to-morrow?"

"I must ask my tutor," he replied.

"Very well, [you can let me know at breakfast

time. I suppose you can find your way to your
part of the house, follow straight along the corridor
till you come to the south wing at the end. Your
study and all the other rooms for you and Dr.
Strickland are there. . Good night."

The next day the ponies were brought round to
the hall door immediately after luncheon, and the
boy and girl were mounted. Cecil, whose chief
mode of locomotion had hitherto been in a palan-
quin, did not by any means enjoy his present situation; but as he made no remark, his cousin supposed
he was as pleased and jubilant at having an oppor-
tunity of seeing the beautiful surroundings of the
place as she was showing them. They rode through
the park, down the long avenue of oaks and beeches,
and out by the keeper's lodge to the lake, and then
away over the hill among the scattered cottages
of the peasants, who touched their hats or cour-
tesied as the cousins rode by. Anna always returning their salutations with some pleasant word
or nod, or an inquiry after their welfare. At last
they turned their ponies homeward. The boy all
the while silent ; the girl chattering and explaining
and repeating anecdotes which had been told to
her, and laughing merrily at the ludicrous passages
in them. As they were again entering the park,
the boy's riding whip slipped out of his hand and
fell to the ground. Looking at his cousin with a
grave expression of face, he said,

" I have dropped my whip, what shall I do ? "

" Dismount and pick it up," replied Anna.

" But I cannot," he replied, "I am afraid I could
not mount again without the groom to help me."

"Very well, then I will get it," so down she sprang, passed up the whip to Cecil, and bounding into her saddle again was off at a canter before the boy could say a word.

"Come along, Cecil," she cried, looking back, "come along, this is the finest stretch of ground in the country for a race."

CHAPTER III.

No—that hallowed form is ne'er forgot
    Which first love traced;
Still it lingering haunts the greenest spot
      On memory's waste.
        'Twas odor fled
        As soon as shed:
'Twas morning's wingèd dream;
'Twas a light that ne'er can shine again
      On life's dull stream:
Oh! 'twas light that ne'er can shine again
      On life's dull stream.

D R. Strickland and his pupil had been fairly ensconced, and for some time past settled in the pretty, sunny rooms in the south wing of the manor house. All the windows of the lower suite opened to the ground, and overlooked and led into a Dutch flower garden, which, in accordance with its name, was laid out in formal walks with high box borders on each side, and stiffly-shaped flower beds of poppies, and tulips, and marigolds, and clusters of monkshood, and the tall white lilies of France, edged round with thyme and sweet bazil. ·In the soft green turf, were planted evergreen trees, which were cut and clipped into fantastic shapes of peacocks, and pyramids, and cubes, and swans, and other devices. Here and there were clumps of holly and yew, from the midst of which some fawn or dryad, some Hebe or Flora, in Italian marble, had long kept watch. Then there were the old cedars of Lebanon, with seats encircling their great trunks, the ends of their long branches lying on the grass, offering beneath them, rest and shade at any hour of the day. The western side of the garden terminated in what was known as Lady Dorothy's walk. A straight, long, gravel walk, bordered on either side by a few feet of soft turf, and an avenue of yew trees two centuries old. The small closely-growing foliage of these trees was so dense that it formed a perpetual green wall, effectually shutting out all the world, with the exception of the sun at noonday, and the stars and moon at night. At the head of the walk was a sundial, and at the further end a fountain. Not a great, noisy, conspicuous construction, suggestive of the rush and turmoil of life, drowning in its splash all the sweet sounds of bird and bee, and the marvelous music of nature, but a pure, gentle, dainty little fountain, the sound of whose crystal drops, so full of soothing and tenderness, fell upon the ear like the voice of the one we love. Near the fountain was a rustic seat from which one might look across the park with its forest trees, its green undulations, and its lake, and still further away westward to the purple Welsh mountains. In every way this was a beautiful garden, a place to dream of, and live, and love, and die in.

Springtime had come, and Cecil and his tutor were sitting in their study, looking out at the linnets flitting about the garden, and at the primroses and blue violets which grew in front of the

windows. The lessons of the day were over, and
the Doctor was pursuing his favorite amusement,
namely, drawing mathematical deductions, and
coming to logical conclusions upon all matters.
Although he was a ripe scholar, he would frequently forget himself, and break out in his strong Scotch
accent; but that signified nothing, as Cecil perfectly
understood his speech, and the family all liked him,
for they knew he was a good man and greatly inter-
ested in the well-doing of his pupil.

"Ye had a lang walk wi' your cousin this morning, " said the Doctor. " I hope ye understand her
better than ye did."

"I am not sure that I do," answered Cecil.   " I
don't see why she moves so quickly and is always
well ; I don't like people who are always well, they
cannot feel for others."

"Ye should no say that, Cecil, when ye look at
your aunt; she's no invalid, but she gi'es up her life
for the sak' o' others. Did ye ken that these verra
rooms are the anes she likes most, the anes she
lived in till we came, and she gave them up that
ye might enjoy the best she had to offer?"

" O yes, I know that," said Cecil.   " My aunt is
very kind, but I was not thinking of her when I
spoke, I was thinking of Cousin Anna ; she runs
so fast and when she is not singing, she is laughing, and I don't believe she has any nerves, for the
other day my pony got a stone in his shoe, and she
was off hers in a moment, seized my pony's fetlock
and snatching up something in the road, knocked
out the stone and mounted in less time than I have

taken to tell you. Now none of the young ladies
in India would take a pony's fetlock in their hand,
so I think Cousin Anna cannot possess nerves."

"In one respect ye are right," said the Doctor,
"Such a young leddie as ony o' those we used to
see in India, would ride on and leave ye, and when
she got home, she would tell one of the servants
to tell some one of the other servants to see aboot
it, and when they had passed the order through
half a dozen, in the course of a few hours perhaps
one of them would be with you, and, in the meantime, she would be lying on the sofa, with Shastri
standing by, fanning her out of her nervous shock."

"But think of the first day I rode with my
cousin, she surprised me so when she picked up
my whip, I thought then she had no nerves."

"Admitting such a statement to be true," replied the Doctor, "which we are by nae means
sure of, for the truth has no been logically proved,
I say, admitting that it be true, is it no' a gude
thing for ye that your cousin has nae nerrves, if ye
are to gang aboot drapping things that ye dar' na
pick up again. In the sense that ye appear to desire
your cousin to hae nerrves, I dinna ken mysel' what
use they wad be to a young leddie wi a speerit such
as she has. I wad no' wish to see a lassie o' her
years hae nerrves; na, na, she wad no hae ony use
for them; Providence kens what is guide for us a',
and will send her the nerrves when she is fit to
manage them."

"Still I don't see," said Cecil, "why she is not
frightened sometimes. Perhaps she may be, but

if so she will never say so ; I don't think a girl
ought to be so fearless."

"Perhaps ye dinna ken that young leddies o'
her rank in England are all educated in that way.
The English hae this proverb amang them. 'A well-
born woman is ever brave.' Your cousin inherits
her courage a long way back, she is no mongrel
born ; I wish ye to see for yourself, Cecil, that it is
a gude thing to be brave. There are mony ways
o' showing it beside being a soldier or a sailor."
And then the Doctor dropped his Scotch accent
and spoke slowly, "We ought to be brave enough
to do our duty to others," said he. "And now I
will give you six reasons for being brave for the
sake of those we love. Firstly, brave that we may
inspire them with courage when their hearts are
weary. Secondly, brave that we may be patient
and gentle when their nerves demand rest. Thirdly
brave that we may be kind and diligent and
loving when they are sick. Fourthly, brave that
we may not be morbid and gloomy and thus de-
press them. Fifthly, brave that we may be faithful and true in all things. Sixthly, brave that we
may endure without murmuring to the end."

Long after the Doctor had left the room, Cecil
was still there, leaning his head against the side of
the window and thinking over this conversation.
He possessed a generous disposition, and could not
bear the idea of having misjudged his cousin. But
he was of a sensitive temperament and not having
a robust constitution, the girl's gaiety of spirit and
great vital energy fatigued him. The cousins con-

tinued their amusements and their studies steadily together for the next two years, and although Cecil still called Anna as wild as a hawk, yet he never got into any serious difficulty, but he applied to her to help him out of it, whether it was in solving a problem or otherwise; carrying out Dr. Strickland's teaching he appeared to feel that his strength lay with her and she in her turn was rejoiced to help him.

There are natures which seem made to help others, they find their greatest happiness in it; and so it was with Anna, the more he needed her help the more she delighted in giving it. Cecil's health was greatly improved by the climate of England, and with stronger health came stronger nerves. He now no longer thought his cousin without them, but he thought she knew how to control them; in fact, they had grown to love each other with that certain kind of cousinly affection which one often sees, and which is very true and lifelong, but has not the rapture, the intensity, nor the anguish, which belong to really falling in love.

It was a day in sweet summer time, all roses and beauty, when the young people met as usual in Lady Dorothy's walk; it was their favorite place, and here they would ramble up and down, and sit by the fountain, and talk, and paint, and read for hours together; and the next day it was the same thing, and the next, and the next, for they never grew tired of the place, or of each other. They were now pacing the long walk, and although they

were past the age of eighteen, they still continued
their studies, but were permitted to select them.

"What a pleasant thing it is, Cecil, to follow out
one's own life and study what we wish," said
Anna. "I am so glad to be free, no more con-
struing sentences, no more conjugating verbs, no
more solving problems; I always hated all of that
dry stuff."

"What are you going to do, then," inquired
Cecil.

"Firstly, I shall spend more time with my
mother, more time in the study of my music, and
read all the poetry I wish to, and ride on horse-
back, and dance, and, of course, help my mother
more in taking care of the peasantry."

"Now, Cecil, what shall you do?"

"Firstly, I think I shall paint, and rove about
among this beautiful scenery," he replied. "I
shall paint until I feel sure that I shall take the
first prize in the grand exhibition; I will not ex-
hibit one stroke of my brush until then."

"Well done, Cecil," said Anna, "that is the
spirit I like."

For she knew as she looked at him, that he
possessed a wealth which no money can buy, a
soul full of poetry, a mind full of genius, the ele-
ments of true greatness in any art, and the only
wealth that she valued.

And Cecil went on with his painting, and pro-
gressed, and brought more depth of tone and
beauty into his pictures with every fresh attempt,
till the canvas seemed to live under his hand, and

his poetic soul and gentle nature spoke through his art. When any difficulty presented itself, he would always seek Anna and have her near him, not that she was an artist, but from some cause he could paint his best when she was by; indeed they were together the greater part of the time, for if they began the day in their different parts of the house, by some chance they either found each other in the library, or Lady Dorothy's walk, long before noon. They drifted to the same place, they scarely knew how, but they began to know that the presence of each one to the other, was equally essential to their happiness. Cecil was a poet, not a writer of rhymes or jingles, but as we have said a true poet in his soul. Anna felt this in all her intercourse with him and heard it in the tones of his voice when he spoke, a voice that had a ring in it, a resonance, and that exquisite power of modulation which says more than the words themselves. And so time went swiftly and sweetly by with their walks and rides, and occupations, until they were twenty years old. Anna happy in the possession of Cecil's love, with life as she wished it, pure, joyous life, with music and beauty everywhere. A song ever on her lips, the happiest, merriest maiden in all " Merrie England."

Cecil in his gentle way, deriving extreme pleasure from the study and exercise of his art, and Anna's companionship. For the cousinly affection of two years ago, had in both of them merged into deep intense love, which ended only with their lives.

CHAPTER IV.

And those were sudden partings such as press
The life from out young hearts.

O who wad wear a silken gown
   Wi' a poor broken heart,
And what 's to me a siller crown
   If from my love I part.

Alone, alone, all, all alone,
   Alone on a wide, wide sea!
And never a saint took pity on
   My soul in agony.

IT was springtime again, and the snowdrops were nodding their dainty, little white heads, and the linnets were again building their nests in the sweet old garden, when Anna's mother summoned her from Cecil's side in Lady Dorothy's walk, to the oak-paneled drawing-room.

"My daughter," she began, "I regret that I must interrupt your present happiness, but circumstances compel me to separate you and Cecil for the present. It is time that you were presented at court, and it is time that you passed a season in London. We have hitherto lead so secluded a life that your name is not known beyond the limits of our county, and I feel I am not doing my duty by you."

"But we are all very happy, mother," said Anna. "Why need we be more known?"

"Yes, my daughter, we are happy now but changes must come to all sometime. I may be called away from you."

"O my dearest mother do not say that, I cannot, I dare not think of what life would be without you; you know I will do anything you wish, or give up everything else in life, but I cannot give you up; it would break my heart, I should die," cried Anna.

"Broken hearts don't die, my daughter, would to God that they did; few, very few die of broken hearts, but many live with them. I have carefully considered what is my duty toward you, and my reason and affection coincide; now listen, in case I am called away by death, there is Cecil to whose care and protection I could resign you, for I knew you loved each other long before you knew it yourselves; I am happy that it is so, but if Cecil were taken away also, there would be no very near relatives to care for you, for the nearest members of your father's family are in India, and mine in the colony of Virginia, and as you will inherit the landed estates of your late grandfather as well as mine, it would be better that you should make trustworthy friends before I leave you, I see this pains you, dear daughter, I shall say no more on this subject. In three days we shall set out for London as the season has already begun, and we shall require some time to get our court dresses made."

The last evening at the manor house was passed by Anna and Cecil under the light of the stars, in Lady Dorothy's walk. The next morning saw the

large, old yellow family coach at the door, drawn by
four strong, heavy horses, a coachman and groom
on the box, a maid and a butler in the rumble, and
the widow and her daughter inside. Cecil who was
standing by one of the coach windows looking very
pale and ·thoughtful, tried to put on a smile as he
said,

" We are to look for you both back again in the
early autumn, you said, aunt."

"Yes, Cecil, as soon as the first brown leaves
fall."

The young people looked good by to each other,
but said not a word, and the heavy old coach
moved away.   In three days more the travelers
were in London, and in due course Anna was presented at court by her mother, who had herself been
presented on the occasion of her marriage.   Then
came calls and cards and invitations to balls and
routs and state dinners, and the poor tired mother
went through all these ceremonies as a duty
toward her daughter, and the daughter endured it
because she loved her mother, and desired to obey
her wish.   It was necessary that a young heiress
of her rank should be dressed in accordance with
the fashion of the day, but the young heiress
longed to be released from the thraldom of fashion,
the fatiguing, heavy brocade dresses, the hoops, the
stiff ruff and the stomacher, the farthingale and high
heeled shoes, and a thousand times more than all,
did she desire to be released from the artificial and
to her unsatisfactory life, from the flattery, the
coquetry, the idle, envious tattle, and to be back

again with Cecil, in her simple, healthy attire, and to live among honest hearts.

The autumn came, and the dry brown leaves began to fall from the trees. Day after day, Cecil opened the harpsichord, and laid a bouquet of the rich deep-hued flowers of the season upon it, and then he took his place by the fountain, and watched the winding road through the park, so that he might get the first sight of the coach when it returned. The autumn leaves continued to fall, and Cecil kept his daily vigil until they were lying deep on the ground, and the branches overhead were bare. Then came a letter saying that Cecil's aunt was ordered by her doctor to pass the winter in Italy, in the hope of curing a cough, which had of late settled upon her, so that it would be spring before the ladies could return to the manor house, hence they traveled to Italy and spent the winter among its masterpieces of genius, both in music and art. The soft air seemed all that was wanted to restore Anna's mother to health. Every day, they found something beautiful that they desired Cecil to see, but it was too late now to send for him, for spring was near. With the spring, came back the cough, and again the medical order was change of climate. This time, a sojourn of some months in Norway was prescribed for Mrs. Vyvyan, bracing air, and much out-door life in the pine woods. After many weeks of slow journeying, the ladies with two of their servants reached Norway, and took up their abode in an old chateau, in the midst of a pine forest so-called, but a forest really composed of many varieties of fir and spruce, as well as pine. The combined aroma of these woods made the air fragrant for many acres around the chateau, and for a time, it appeared to have the most beneficial effect upon the invalid. But one quiet eve, when the summer days had waned, and the faded leaves of another autumn fell, a pang of anguish shot through Anna's heart. The dearly loved mother was called away.

. . . .

A short time only had elapsed since that event, and the servants were packing, and making preparations for the return to the manor house, when a mounted courier arrived at the chateau, with a large package of papers addressed in Dr. Strickland's handwriting. Very long, and full of feeling, and minute in every detail, was the letter the good man had written, if letter so long a dispatch might be called. He told of Cecil's conversations, of his watchings from beside the fountain; how every day he picked flowers, and put them on the harpsichord, saying this is the place she loves best; and how he faded and wasted day by day, yet struggled so bravely against the hand of death, that he might finish his last and best picture for Anna; and how on the last day of his life, he had laid his flowers on the harpsichord as usual, and then desired to be carried to the library and lifted into their great-grandfather's chair to die,—the chair that Anna had placed for him the first time they met.

When Anna had finished reading the final words of Dr. Strickland's letter, she rose and moved quietly into the recess of one of the large, heavily mullioned windows, and looked down a long vista into the forest, to the tall dark pines under which was her mother's grave. Every vestige of color had left both cheek and lip, and she stood in the great somber room, as cold and white and as still as the statues which adorned its walls. The extremes of grief and joy have no speech ; she had none. No cry of lamentation went forth ; no tears of relief fell from her eyes ; she knew her life was ended, but she also knew that she could not die. Three words only escaped her lips. "O God, alone."

CHAPTER V.

Has hope like the bird in the story,
  That flitted from tree to tree
With the talisman's glittering glory
  Has hope been that bird to thee?

On branch after branch alighting,
  The gem did she still display,
And when nearest and most inviting,
  Then waft the fair gem away?

MONG the papers of the late mistress of the manor house, were found two letters which from their dates showed that they had been written during her stay in Italy. One was addressed to Sir Thomas Richardson, Lord Chief Justice of England, the other to her daughter. She appeared to have had a foreshadowing of her death, and directed Anna, in case of such an event, to have Sir Thomas' letter delivered to him immediately, and to abide by whatever decision he might come to. Anna had never seen Sir Thomas, but she knew that he was in some way related to her on her mother's side of the family, and that he was an old gentleman, who lived among his books, in an old-fashioned country house in one of the midland counties of England, with no one but his servants about him. And when the decision came, which informed Miss Vyvyan that she too was to live there, as his ward, she was

thankful, for the tie of kindred was strong in her
nature, and she thought to herself, there is still a
link, that connects with the memory of my loved
mother. Besides he is old and alone, perhaps I
may be able to do something to make his life less
lonely. But what could she do, she asked herself,
for to her all seemed vague and undefined.

Arriving at the quiet old home of Sir Thomas,
with its smooth green lawn and flat meadows
around and in front of the house, she was shown
into the presence of a tall, stately, white-haired,
old gentleman to whom nature had indeed been
gracious, for he was extremely handsome, and of
courtly manners. He greeted her kindly but with
much dignity, and addressed her throughout the
conversation as Miss Vyvyan. A shudder swept
through her frame each time she heard herself so
called, by the only one left who had the right to
address her by her own familiar name of Anna,
which she had hoped he would do. But although
desiring to be in every way kind to his ward, his
ideas of dignity and courtesy were fixed, and to
him she was always Miss Vyvyan. Thus without
a thought of causing her pain, he ever brought
before her the deepest sense of her bereavement
and her isolation. Life in Sir Thomas' home was
very different from life at the manor house, both
in doors and out. The old gentleman passed most
of his time in his library, and Anna rarely saw him
until evening, when he would sometimes instruct
her in playing chess. When she went outside
of the house, all seemed strange and dull and

dreary, plain grass lawns all around, not a flower bed to be seen, no long garden walk, no fountain, no hills to ramble over, no purple mountains in the distance, but a flat level country on all sides. And when she came in doors again, no loved mother, no Cecil to greet her.

Nearly three years had gone by since Anna's arrival as Sir Thomas' ward. It was evening, and they had just finished their game of chess, when he for the first time addressed her as my dear young lady, and after a short pause proceeded.

"This is not a fit place for you; I am too old to be the companion of youth; I am doing you injustice in allowing you to remain with me, and have decided that you shall have a more suitable home."

"I do not wish to leave you, Sir Thomas," replied Anna, "besides I have nowhere to go. I cannot live at the manor house all alone."

"Certainly you cannot," he answered. "I have arranged everything for you to the best of my power. You do not really come into property until you are twenty-five years of age. Your landed estates and other moneys are secured to you in such a way that you need not feel the least apprehension about your affairs, everything has been attended to. The manor house will be in the charge of a steward for the present. You will probably wish to live there again some day. As I have just said, I am too old; I may not, I cannot have long to remain here. There is a cousin of your mother living in the colony of Virginia, Fairfax by name. He has a wife and family, two nephews,

whom he has adopted, twins, I think, also Fairfaxes.
They stand in the degree of a third generation
from myself. I mean to say these twins are about
the same age my grandson would be now, had he
been spared to my declining years. Therefore,
they must be a few years older than you are, and
more adapted for being companionable to you,
than I am. I have been in correspondence with
your Cousin Fairfax, during many months, in
regard to your making your home with them in
Virginia, until you are older, and have ceased so
much to need protection, or until you have settled
in a home of your own. The arrangement appears
to be very agreeable to them, and I trust you will
· be happy in their society. I cannot part with you
without saying that your presence in my house
has given me much pleasure—the only one now left
to me, that of recollection. Although you are very
quiet, for one who has only reached your years, yet
the sound of your footstep about the house called
sweet though sad memories of my only daughter,
and I thank you for them. If I thought only of
myself, I should keep you here till the end, but
there are times when it is more noble to resign
than to fulfill the dearest wishes of our heart."

. . . .

It was in the summer of 1607 that Miss Vyvyan,
attended by her waiting woman, sailed from England, for the colony of Virginia, in the ship Queen
Elizabeth, from which she had just been wrecked,
when we took up the narrative of her early life.
To that period of time we will now return.

CHAPTER VI.

This is the forest primeval. The murmuring pines and the
    hemlocks,
Bearded with moss, and in garments green, indistinct in the
    twilight.
Stand like Druids of eld, with voices sad and prophetic.
Stand like harpers hoar with beards that rest on their bosoms.
Loud from its rocky caverns the deep-voiced neighboring ocean,
Speaks and in accents disconsolate answers the wail of the forest.

    And thou too who so 'ere thou art
      That readest this brief psalm
    As one by one thy hopes depart
      Be resolute and calm.

    Oh fear not in a world like this,
      And thou shalt know ere long,
    Know how sublime a thing it is
      To suffer and be strong.

AS the shipwrecked young lady lay on the
cold, rough beach, amid the dead bodies,
with the hoarse roar of the ocean sounding in her ears, and the heavy, wet clouds
of mist clinging about her, indifferent to life or
death, the recollection of the ship being pursued
by buccaneers and driven far out of her course
came back to her mind, and then being caught in
a hurricane and seeing another vessel battling with
the tempest, and both ships furiously hurried on
toward a wild, rocky coast, the vessels crashing on
shore and rebounding again, and some one lifting

her into a boat, and then she remembered no more. While these recollections were passing through her brain, she raised herself upon her elbow and looked around. Death everywhere, the ocean with its floating corpses and wreckage lay before her. On either hand a long broken beach, with its gloomy rocks and its scattered dead. A scene which at any other time in her life would have struck her with awe, she now gazed at quietly, and questioned "Why am I the only one left, oh, if I too could die." Turning to look behind her through the mist, she observed that the land was hilly, and in some places rose to a considerable height. The whole surface as far as she could make out was covered by a thick growth of lofty pines, mingled with spruce and other sorts of fir, among which sprung up an entanglement of various kinds of undergrowth, all these trees and shrubs growing nearly down to the sea and forming so thick a forest, that it was impossible for sight to penetrate it further than a few yards. There was no building of any kind to be seen, no sign of human habitation of either savage or civilized life. The great abundance of pine trees, and the general appearance of the forest, which strongly resembled the forests of Norway, instantly called up the question in Anna Vyvyan's mind, can it be possible that destiny has sent me back to the land of my mother's grave?

A low wail like the cry of a young child in distress, caused the only hearer to start to her feet, and looking on the other side of a broken rock close by, she saw stretched out white and still, a young lady by the side of whom, in a half-standing position, and bending over her was a beautiful golden-haired little girl of between two and three years. In another instant Anna was also bending over the young mother, to whom she found the child was tied by a crimson silk sash such as were worn by military officers. The tearful little one turned up her sweet face, without any apparent fear, but with a great deal of sorrow in it, and said, in her baby language,

" Mama dorn seep," then she pressed her lips upon the cold white cheek, and kissed it and stroked and patted the also beautiful mother, who lay so mute and pallid and unconscious of all her little one's gentle love.

Again and again came the cry from the poor forlorn little creature, " Det up, mama, det up, mama ;" but the dear mamma was beyond the reach of the sweet baby voice. Anna's first thought was to see if any sign of life remained in the slender form before her, but she could find no pulse, and the face and hands were as cold, as the rocks upon which she was lying. Miss Vyvyan unfastened the child, and drew away the long sash, which had tied her to her mother's waist. As she did so, she observed the delicately formed features, which were so regular and proportionate that they might have been chiseled in marble, to represent some Greek goddess. She saw the masses of soft brown hair, and the long dark eyelashes, which dropped upon the cheek like silken fringe. She observed, too, the simple traveling habit, made of the finest material, but perfectly free from any attempt at vulgar ornament. And as she took the child into her arms, and looked down once more on the sweet white face, which lay on the stones at her feet, and noted the refinement in everything about her, she knew that the little one's mother came of gentle blood. The child was willing to go to Anna, but not willing to be removed out of sight of its mother. So Miss Vyvyan sat down where they were with the little one in her lap, and shook out the silk sash with the idea of wrapping it round the shivering child, but that, too, was wet, every thing in the shape of clothing was wet, both on Anna and the child. All that she could do for the moment to comfort the tiny thing, was to fold it in her arms, and try by that means to keep it from perishing with cold. It had probably been shielded by some heavy woolen wrap, which was torn off by the breakers when they were cast on shore, for as Anna shook out the silk sash, there fell from it a strip of thick woolen fringe, which had the appearance of having belonged to a shawl.

But now the child was bareheaded, and wore a little white dress of exceedingly fine embroidery, which also spoke of the mother's love, for none but loving hands ever wrought work so dainty as that. Round its neck was clasped a small gold chain of minute links of very fine workmanship. So thin and delicately was it made, that it resembled a thread of golden silk. Anna examined it carefully to see if she could find any letter or name upon it,

but none was there, then she spoke to the child as
it lay nestling its pretty head upon her arm, and
still talking to its mother, and said,

"Tell me, dear little one, what is your name?"

The child looked up, but evidently could not
understand the meaning of her words.

Anna tried again by laying one of her fingers on
the child's shoulder and saying, " Who's dat?"

"Mama's baby," answered the little one in an
instant.

" Will Mama's baby tell me where papa is?"

" Dorn seep," replied the child.

" Tell me where dorn seep, sweet child."

" Down dare," answered she, pointing to a mass
of human bodies which were thrown together on
the beach some distance below them, and which
were constantly kept in motion by the incoming
tide.

Anna's desire to die no longer existed; as she
held the beautiful little creature to her heart and
rocked it, all her thoughts concentrated in the one
question, what could she do to aid this sweet help-
less one. The ideas rushed through her mind
with the rapidity that they come to us in fever. It
must have warmth and food, or it will perish. I
cannot let it die, it is so beautiful, and I love it. I
must act this moment. Rising with the child in
her arms, she hastened along as rapidly as she
could among the wreckage, scrambling between
bales and chests of all kinds, in the hope of finding something, anything; she could not surmise
what it might be, but some sustenance must be

had for the child. Although hundreds of cases and bales were strewed about, they were all so securely corded and nailed up, that it was impossible to procure anything from them.

At last, far in on the land, she came to a large pile of freight, which had struck so violently, that the greater number of the cases and bales, had broken in two, or had burst open. The first object that met her sight, was a broken chest full of table covers of rich cloth, evidently the product of India and Persia, as the silk embroidered borders in oriental needlework showed; happily everything was thrown in so far that it was dry.

Taking one of the table covers, she wrapped it round the child, who in the midst of its discomfort showed its gentle nature by saying,

" Pitty sing, pitty sing," and holding up its sweet face to kiss Anna.

" Yes, mama's baby shall have more pretty things soon," said Miss Vyvyan.

"Dinner," cried the child, "bing dinner, Dinah bing dinner."

" Yes, darling, we must find dinner for mama's baby."

" Dinah bing dinner?" again repeated the poor, hungry little thing, with an expressive look of interrogation.

" Yes, dear, yes ;" folding the soft woolen cover still more closely round the child, Anna placed her in a sheltered spot: " Stay there a moment, baby, while I bring dinner."

From the marks on the outside of the boxes it

was plain that they had come from some Mediter-
ranean port, and contained fruits and other edibles.
With a heavy stone, Anna soon broke open a small
box of candied fruit, selecting some, she gave it to
the half-starved child. One of the baby hands
held her fruit, the other one was instantly stretched
out toward the box,

"Mama, tandy, too " she cried.

" Mama is asleep, darling, she does not want
candy,"

" Oh mama, tandy, too," she repeated, with an
earnestness that sent a thrill through Anna's heart.

" Yes ; mama's baby shall take some if she wishes
to."

The child took a piece of the fruit, " Doe now,"
she said.

"Go where, baby ? "

" Mama," answered the child, struggling among
the folds of her wrap, to get on to her feet and
pointing in the direction of its mother. A nature
so full of love, shall not be pained or thwarted by
me, mused Anna, as she carried back the child
who had already become precious to her. When
they reached the place where the cold white mother
was lying, and Anna was in the act of putting the
little one on the ground as it desired, an unusually
large wave broke so close by, that the spray and
foam dashed against, and flowed over the sweet
pale face. The child uttered a sharp cry of distress, and disengaging itself from Anna's arms and
darting to its mother, threw itself down by her
side, and, clasping her neck with its tiny arms,

covered with kisses the face that was so dear.
The next wave will carry the mother away, Anna
thought. I cannot let the child witness such a
sight, it would break her loving little heart, and
she also felt that she, herself, could not give up to
the all-devouring ocean, the object of so much
affection in the babe. Placing the little one in
safety, she took up the the cold, white burden in
her arms, and carried it far back from the reach of
the sea, putting it down on the moss, at the root of
a large pine. As it lay there so lone and sad and
beautiful, with the child standing by it, for the
little soul had followed with its swiftest steps,
Anna bent over it and kissed the face. Poor dear,
she murmured in a whisper, as long as I exist, my
love and my life shall be devoted to your child.
She bent again and kissed the cold lips. Could it
be possible that breath came lightly through them?
It was, — it was,— deeper and deeper drawn and
more regular each time. Merciful God, she lives,
and the tears fell fast from eyes that had long been
dry with grief. A faint sigh, and the partial part-
ing of the long silken eyelashes, told that life was
coming back still more and more. In a few
moments she feebly uttered, "My child."

"Your child is safe and with you," replied Anna,
lifting the little one closer to its mother's side.

"Dudley," she faltered.

"He has not come yet," said Anna, surmising
for whom she was inquiring, and pitying in her
inmost soul the widowed heart that must so soon
learn to live without him.

When the poor mother opened her eyes, the scene of horror was more than her delicate organization could endure, and a violent fit of trembling came upon her.

" Tote on," said the anxious, sensitive child.

The suggestion was acted upon, Anna ran to the pile of dry wreckage, and soon returned with an armful of table covers and a box.

"Tote on mama," cried the child hurriedly, as if it felt there was no time to be lost.

" Yes, darling, a coat for mama," said Anna, improvising a pillow with one, and wrapping several other warm covers about the shivering mother.

" Take this," said she, holding to her lips some cordial which she had poured into a mussel shell, " It is buanaba, a very delicate restorative made in Turkey, pray try to take it, it will keep you from shivering so."

As we have already said, Anna possessed great vital energy, and with her to think was to act. She saw that the delicate, slender young mother and the child must both die, unless she could find some means of getting them warm. There was an abundance of dead wood close by, if she could only start the first spark of fire. Pushing her way a few yards into the forest, she brought out a quantity of dead grass and resinous wood, and continued striking two stones together until at last the spark came, and a good fire soon blazed high, and sent out its glow toward the pine tree beneath which they were lying. Some large stones were soon heated in the hot embers, and rolled to the feet of the mother. Covering was brought and held to the fire, and the lowly bed made so warm that the exhausted mother and her little one fell into a natural and refreshing sleep. In the meantime Anna was everywhere scrambling and climbing among the freight, dragging what she could not carry, searching for anything that might be appropriated as a covering against the cold, and looking after the cases of eatables with a thought for the poor, starving ones under the pine tree. It was late in the afternoon when the sleepers awoke. The mist had in a great measure cleared away, and the sunlight was struggling through the remaining clouds. A good fire was burning, and a tin of water was boiling beside it. A long box cover, supported by stones at each end, formed a table, other box lids made seats, and the table was spread with food that would at least sustain life. Heaped up under another pine tree, was a sufficient supply of both food and covering, to provide for the ladies and child for some time to come. There was no lack of tins of all shapes, so they were made use of to cook in, and for holding food. As soon as the child was thoroughly awake, it sat up in its bed, showing its sweet fair face, and · smiling with happiness at finding its mother awake by its side. Taking up a cup of food made from sea moss and sweetened with the candied fruit, Anna attempted to feed the child by means of a shell, but it turned its face away, and said in tones full of distress, "Mama too, Dinah bing dinner." When Anna took hot coffee from the fire and

propped up the exhausted mother and induced her
to drink it, everything went well with the child.
It was perfectly satisfied, and took its own food,
and laughed and played with the pebbles and
shells that were brought to it.

"I have tried often, very often to speak to you,"
said the mother, addressing Anna for the first time;
"I was conscious, but I could not speak; I was too
weak I suppose, and now my voice has come back
to me, I have no words, I do not know what I
can say to you."

"Will you let me suggest what you shall say,"
asked Anna? "It is this; say what I can do that
would most help you and your lovely child; and
now try to rest while I think how you can be sheltered from the night air, for night will be upon us
in the course of two hours at furthest."

The fog and mist had now completely disappeared, and given way to the sun, which, however,
was nearing the horizon, and the trees cast long
shadows on the grass.

While the mother and child had been asleep in
the afternoon, Anna had built up a few broken
boards and stones between them and the sea, that
they might not be pained on their first awaking by
seeing the terrible sight which was so near.

"I am better," said the mother. "I feel stronger.
I cannot endure to see you doing all. I want to
help you. I do not need more rest now. But tell
me first, pray tell me the truth, whatever it may
be. Is there any one left alive here besides our-
selves. Have you seen an officer in a colonel's

uniform? My husband was in the service of King James, he wore the royal uniform, when he tied my child to my waist with his sash, and lifted me into a boat. I cannot remember any more. I think I must have been stunned. How long have we been here? I seem to have lost some of the time, but I felt you take away my child, and I heard you speak tenderly to it. Have we been here too long for my husband to be living? Tell me, can it be possible that I may find him?"

Anna could not add to her anguish by repeating what the child had said when questioned about its father, for she believed it had spoken truly when it answered,

"Dorn seep, down dare."

"I do not think we have been here longer than to-day," she replied. "I do not know exactly. It was early in the morning when our ship struck the rocks, but it was broad daylight when I came to my senses on the shore. The tide was coming in, it was very high, and now it must have been going out for nearly four hours, so I think we must have been cast on shore this morning."

"Then my husband may still be alive, I must seek him." With those words, she rose to her feet, but nearly fainted with the effort.

"Your child is sleeping," said Anna. "Let me support you, if you will attempt to walk. Tell me your husband's name, that I may call it aloud; these rocks are very rugged and I can send my voice into places among them, that it would be impossible to go into."

3

"Colonel Carleton," she replied.

"Lean on me, Mrs. Carleton. Shall we go down this way?"

The tide had carried out the mass of floating bodies to which the child had pointed at noon, but numbers of others still remained in all directions. Tottering and staggering among the dead, Mrs. Carleton continued her search, until she had looked into every ghastly face that lay there.

"Now will you call aloud for me," she said, "for I cannot, my strength is gone."

Anna called, but the only sound that came back was the echo of her own voice from the forest and the heavy rolling of the sea. They returned in silence to the child, who was still asleep. The sun had nearly set, when all at once a rich, bright glow from the west rose behind the forest and flooded every object with golden light. Looking out to sea eastward, they observed only a few miles away many islands, some of them covered with forests down to the water's edge.

"Where can we be," they both ejaculated at the same time. There was no habitation visible on any of them, nor any smoke rising from them.

"These trees remind me of Norway," said Anna. "Do you think we can be in Norway?"

"I am unable to say," replied Mrs. Carleton, "but I am sure we are in a northern clime by the growth both of trees and plants."

The ladies seated themselves by the sleeping child, trying to think what it was best for them to do. There was no time for delay; it would soon be dark, and the little group of three appeared to be the only living human beings in the place, wherever that place might be. While they were talking together, they had turned their backs to the sea and were looking toward the sunset, and watching the varied rays of light which here and there penetrated through the forest on the hill before them.

"I did not hear your name, Mrs. Carleton, on board the ship I sailed in from England," said Anna.

"I did not come from England" she answered. "My parents settled in the colony of Virginia long ago. I was born there, that is my home. My husband as well as myself, had many relatives in England, and we were going to visit them, and intended to have our child baptized there, that its name might be registered among those of its forefathers. Sometime after we sailed, we fell in with buccaneers ; but our ship, the Sir Walter Raleigh, was a fast sailor, and we got away from them ; yet I was told when the hurricane came on, that they were the cause of our being out of our course, hence our calamity."

"We met the same destiny," said Anna, and then she told in a few words whence she had sailed, and that her name was Vyvyan.

The hill in front of the ladies, rose too high for them to see the actual setting of the sun, but the rich glow of gold and crimson now lit up the whole forest, and defined the outline of the rising ground.

"What is that I see?" said Mrs. Carleton, shading her eyes with her hands.

"Tall pines" I think, answered Anna.

" No, it is a tower ; look, Miss Vyvyan, in that direction, see on the hill ; it is a stone tower ; look, now the light has changed ; there are windows, many of them, see on the right the building extends a great way, it is very large."

Anna looked through the wood where Mrs. Carleton directed, and saw distinctly in the rosy light of the sunset, an immense stone building, with a massive tower capable of containing many rooms, and rising to the height of two hundred feet, With the exception of the tower, the building was very irregular, and gave the impression of having been erected at different periods. It combined the characteristics of a feudal castle and a fortress. It was old and gray, but by no means a ruin, yet it had a gloomy and forbidding appearance. The ladies looked at each other and hesitated, they did not speak for a few moments ; the same idea possessed the mind of each. They thought that good people would not live in such a place, amid such wild surroundings, but neither one of them would unnerve the other by saying so, for they knew in their present situation they required all the courage that they could command, in order that they might be ready to meet their uncertain fate.

While they continued looking almost spellbound the child awoke, and observing their earnest gaze, added her own scrutiny to theirs. She bent her little golden head forward and saw some of the windows upon which the reflection of light glinted.

"Home" she exclaimed, smiling with childish glee, "doe home," taking hold of her mother's dress to draw her in the direction of the building, which was about half-way up the hill, and only a few hundred yards from where they now stood.

CHAPTER VII.

The battled towers the donjon keep,
  The loop-hole grates where captives weep,
The flanking walls that round it sweep,
  In yellow luster shone.

———

Act,—act in the living present!
  Heart within and God o'erhead!

———

Let us then be up and doing
  With a heart for any fate
Still achieving, still pursuing
  Learn to labor and to wait.

HE ladies held a consultation, should they attempt to go to the castle and ask for shelter. How could the child, which like themselves had hitherto lived in luxury, pass a night on the beach. Beside the forest looked as if it was the resort of wolves and bears. It would be unsafe. They could not after dark remain where they were, there was no alternative, so they decided to go at once to the building. There was no path, but they held the branches aside for each other. Taking the child with them, they stumbled over the loose stones and among the briers as well as their want of strength would permit, for they were much exhausted. Mrs. Carleton was so weak that she fell several times and was severely hurt, but no murmur escaped her and she rose and struggled on again as if nothing had happened, turning, from time to time, with some word of kindness or cheer to Miss Vyvyan, who was helping the little one along.

Emerging from the woods, they found themselves in a long, open space of grass, which was surrounded on all sides by the forest. The great building stood full in front of, and overshadowed them. It was a veritable feudal castle and, as we have said, grand, gloomy and forbidding to look at. The windows were far up from the ground, no entrance door was in sight, no walks or drives around it, everywhere rank grass, with here and there a tuft of golden-rod, or fall aster springing up. No smoke rising from any of the chimneys, no traces of footsteps, no sound but the sighing of the wind through the pines, and the surging of the ocean. Mrs. Carleton was first to break the silence.

" If I were by myself," said she, " I should imagine I must be dreaming, but I feel the reality of our position, this is no dream. We are all alone here; this place must have been deserted long ago. Look, there is the entrance overgrown with brambles. It is best that we are alone ; if we can get shelter, we need not fear molestation."

She spoke calmly and cheerfully and tried to wear a smile for the sake of the two who were looking at her and listening to her words. Anna had entertained grave fears for Mrs. Carleton while they were getting up to the castle. She thought the delicate frame must give way altogether, but she now saw that her newly-made friend was as

brave, as she was gentle and loving and faithful,
and fear gave place to hope and resolve. As she
went a few steps to gather some asters, which the
child wished for, she said to herself, " This fragile,
suffering, uncomplaining woman has already taught
me a great lesson, and I will never seek selfish
relief by adding to her overburdened life, the
weight of my own sorrow. She shall always think
me cheerful, whatever I may know my self to be,
for nothing that I can do will be of so much help
to her and the sweet child."

As Anna returned, the little one stretched out
her hands to receive the flowers and held up the
rosy lips to give a kiss for them, which was her
usual mode of acknowledging any kindness shown
to her.

"Miss Vyvyan," said Mrs. Carleton, "I have
been looking on the other side while you have
been gathering the flowers. I find there is an
immense pile of ruins there, which looks as if it
were the ruins of a tower. That small entrance
at the north end is the only one that is open.
Shall we try to get in, we can beat down the
brambles."

The doorway was low and arched, the stone
work about it coarse and massive, the door had
fallen from the upper hinge, and lay so far open
that ingress was very easy. The ladies entered
and passed into a broad stone passage, which was
many yards in length and led to a staircase at the
foot of the great tower at the south end. As they
passed along the passage, they saw a number of

rooms on either side, which were all in semidark-
ness, being lighted only by narrow loopholes in the
outer walls, yet there was sufficient light to show
them that they were all well filled with what
appeared to be chests, boxes and packages, but the
ladies were too much fatigued to make any examination of them. They observed that the walls
were all of rough stone, but there was no feeling
of dampness. On reaching the staircase, Mrs.
Carleton discovered some inscriptions cut deep
into the wall.

"What is this, Miss Vyvyan? I see it is not
Greek or Latin or Hebrew. I never saw any
characters like these." ,

" They are runic," replied Anna. " I should
not know what they are, only that I have seen them
on old ruins in Norway. Do you think we are in
Norway? This old castle is very much like build-
ings I have seen there."

Mrs. Carleton, who was an excellent botanist,
again referred to the trees and plants which they
had seen as they came up from the beach.

" Those fall asters," she said, " and the species
of golden-rod are both of northern growth, but I
cannot in the least feel sure of our whereabouts.
It scarcely seems probable that we shall find the
means of getting away from this place very soon,
for there is no evidence of any commerce here,
and as far as I can judge, nothing for merchants or
traders to come for. I do not say this to dishearten
you, Miss Vyvyan, but I feel it right that we
should speak openly and honestly to each other."

3*

"I understand you" replied Anna, "you do not
wish to fill my imagination with false hopes; it is
good, and kind, and sensible, and I thank you for
speaking as you have done. I feel myself that
this is no time for dreaming, and I do not any
longer care to indulge in it. All I care for, is to
lead an earnest, true life in whatever position Fate
may place me. If we are destined to remain together, you shall see."

The ladies had now ascended the winding stone
staircase as far as the top of the first flight from
the ground. From the stairs, they stepped into a
corridor with a stone floor and bare stone walls,
somewhat similar to the one below, but wider and
well lighted. From this corridor, branched off
other passages and staircases, leading both above
and below, and numberless rooms of all kinds, the
doors of which were chiefly open, showing the
most luxurious and costly furniture, and the richest hangings, containing chests filled with rich vel-
vets and satins, and all other requirements of
ladies' dress. Some rooms were evidently sleeping
apartments, others were furnished as parlors, the
walls being hung with tapestry, and adorned with
rare paintings and mirrors in frames of the most
exquisite workmanship, in ivory, silver and bronze.
Rich carpets and rugs covered the floors. The
rooms all felt dry. They had wide, open fireplaces
in which stood fire dogs of brass or iron ; in some
of them still remained half-burned or charred logs,
and the dead ashes of long years ago. The
ladies remarked that, amidst all this abundance of

wealth, there was a certain incongruity in the arrangement of the contents of every room. In one
they found silk draperies from India, a divan from
Turkey, an Italian settee in the finest Florentine
carving; beside it a massive English table of heart
of oak, and the light, spider-legged gilt chairs of
Paris, with their faded red silk cushions, and so on.
They rambled through room after room. In many
of them were firearms of all dates and nations,
sabers and cutlasses, daggers and swords, with pis-
tols and guns, and powder flasks, and spears.
Some of these lay upon the tables and chairs, and
others hung from the walls. In all the sleeping-
rooms, were numberless articles of men's dress,
uniforms and costumes of various kinds, sufficient
in variety to supply disguises for a whole regiment.
With the exception of the number of firearms
and other instruments of warfare lying about, the
rooms were all in order. The reflection of the setting sun streamed in at the windows, and across
the floors at the west side of the castle, and lit up
the mirrors, and pictures, and beautiful and curious
works of art, which hung on the walls, or stood on
the shelves, or on quaint pieces of furniture, and
which abounded everywhere and made the interior
of the building a pleasant contrast to the gloomy-
looking outside.

Passing hastily through the rooms which led off
the corridors, the ladies returned to the great
tower at the south end. They found the door,
which gave entrance to it was closed; but on Mrs.
Carleton laying her hand upon the lock, it at once

gave way, and they went through a vestibule, and
entered a large and very handsome room. It was
octagon in form, with a window in every division. The upper part of each window was made
of antique painted glass, which shed red hues of
crimson, gold and purple in different parts of the
room, ever varying their position with the change
in the sun's altitude, and giving the apartment at
all times of the day, a bright, cheerful appearance.
This room was furnished still more gorgeously
than any of the others. The walls were hung
with the richest kinds of Spanish tapestry ; on
a ground of dark green silk velvet, was embroidered large flowers and arabesques in gold, interspersed at intervals with the well-known representa-
tions of the three castles, which are a part of the
arms of Spain. The furniture was all of chestnut,
carved in the deeply cut and highly raised work,
which is so rich and elaborate, and peculiar to the
Spanish artists. Several curiously cut mirrors
hung on the walls, and also some exceedingly delicate paintings in ivory, and a number of choice
enamels on plaques of gold. The mantel piece of
stone was high and · adorned with beautiful vases
of Egyptian and Etruscan make, mingled with
those of Rome and Herculaneum, and the more
modern flower-holders of Bohemian and Venetian
glass. The sofas, as well as the luxurious arm-
chairs, were covered with green silk velvet. The
window draperies were of the same, ornamented
with gold fringe.

The floor was made of various kinds, inlaid in

mosaic work, as we see them in Italy. Soft ruby colored rugs were lying in front of the table, and before the fireplace. On one side, was a small carved bookcase containing a few volumes of novels, some of poetry and a few sacred books of the Roman Catholic creed, all of them in Spanish.

In one or two of the books, the name of "Inez" was written. Across the end of one of the sofas lay a guitar of satin-wood, inlaid with mother-o'-pearl, with a Spanish lace mantilla by the side of it, and on a small table close by was an open music book containing Spanish songs.

Everything gave evidence of having been left untouched for many years, the flowers in the vases had dried, and fallen bit by bit, and lay in small heaps that looked like chaff. In one corner of the room stood a tall Chinese jar, that had once contained sprays of the fragrant fir balsam, which was now little else than dust. In the wide, open fireplace on the hearth, the wood that had been carefully placed on the dogs ready to light, had become so dry, that it had crumbled away, and fallen to pieces with its own weight.

The ladies felt the importance of using the remaining daylight in making some preparations for the night, so deferred any further examination of the castle until the next day. They experienced a certain feeling of safety in being alone. .

"Mrs. Carleton," said Miss Vyvyan, "you will not mind if I run down to the beach, and bring up some of the table covers and some food. I shall soon be back again."

"I do not mind being left, but I do mind your doing it without help ; I want to help you in everything, but I am not strong enough yet. We will stand by the window and watch you as far as we can."

The child understood the conversation, and turning with a very earnest and inquiring look to her mother, she said, .

"Be back."

"Yes, dear, Miss Vyvyan is coming back. That is my little one's way of saying she wishes you to return," said Mrs. Carleton. "She always says to me, if I am leaving the room, 'be back,' she means come back."

"I like to hear her say it," said Anna; "it sounds so real and so pretty, and it is her own way of expressing what she desires. I hope you will always allow her to keep that little remnant of babyhood. I ask it of you as a favor."

"I am only too glad, Miss Vyvyan, to do anything you wish," replied Mrs. Carleton.

As Anna left the room and hastened down the tower stairs, she heard the sweet little voice calling after her,

"Be back, be back."

Mrs. Carleton had prepared a pleasant surprise for Anna on her return. She had taken a flint from the lock of one of the guns, and had succeeded in lighting a cheerful fire, before which the ladies spread the table covers, and slept until the light of the morning sun shone in upon them through one of the painted windows, and made brilliant hues in various parts of the room, which the child called butterflies. The little party was rested and refreshed, and awoke to be greeted by a beautiful day.

As soon as they had breakfasted, they began a thorough investigation of their new abode. They descended to the basement where they had entered, and discovered in one of the rooms immense stores of provisions of all kinds, many of them in good order, for they were in sealed jars and cases. One of the down-stairs rooms was a carpenter's shop, containing tools of all sorts, which were of great use to the ladies in opening many things that it would have been impossible for them to do otherwise. There was a large store of wine, and a kitchen containing strangely shaped cooking utensils from different countries. Near the small north doorway by which the ladies entered the castle, was a narrow stone staircase, leading down under ground, but it was so dimly lighted, that they did not attempt to go down it. Ascending again to the tower, they discovered several more beautiful rooms in it, all richly furnished. All these rooms had apparently been set apart for the use of the lady, with the exception of one, a library, containing carved oak shelves, loaded with books in many different languages ; the heavy furniture was also of carved oak, cushioned with old gold embossed leather. A Spanish cloak of crimson velvet was thrown across the back of one of the chairs, and upon the seat of it lay a sombrero with a plume, also a sword and a pair of

gauntlets. An arched doorway in one corner of
the library, led into a small watch tower, the whole
size of which was filled up by a winding stone
staircase.

"Come, Miss Vyvyan," said Mrs. Carleton, "we
will go up here, and we may, perhaps, see something that will tell us where we are." They
climbed the stairs to the top, and passed through a
low door on to the battlements of a great tower,
whence they looked down at the pine trees, two
hundred feet below. They saw at once that they
were on an island ; not by any means a large one,
and that the whole of it was covered by forest as
far as the water's edge, excepting in a few places
where a bare rock or swamp intervened. They
looked to the south and saw only the open ocean.
The day was clear and calm, and they could see
away to the horizon. To the east lay many other
islands ; then to the north the same sight met
their eyes. Looking to the west still more islands
were to be seen, and also what appeared to be the
mainland, and far away, perhaps seventy miles off
in the distance, a magnificent range of lofty mountains. Nothing could exceed the beauty of the
scene. As they walked round the top of the
tower, looking down upon all these forest-clad
islands without any sign of habitation, Mrs. Carleton, turning to Anna, said, " Let us try to think
over all the maps we have studied in our geogra-
phy lessons."

"Just what I have been trying to do," said Anna,
"but I can only think of a great number of islands

in the Pacific ocean, and we know we are not there, and we are not in any of the West India islands, for, as you say, the trees tell us we are in the north, and now that I see so many islands, I know we are not in Norway. But is it not strange that the runic characters are in so many places in this castle? See, here are more of them, exactly the same as I saw when we were in Norway."

" Yes," replied Mrs. Carleton ; " everything tells us we are in the north, and also tells us we are alone. We may have to remain here, we know not how long, perhaps years ; and then, too, we have something else to consider. These trees show that the winters in this region are very severe, as do also the rents in the rocks that we clambered among on our way up to the castle. Those great fissures were all caused by the action of intense frosts, by such a degree of cold as you and I have no idea of, excepting from what we have read. In a climate like this, we know the winter sets in early, so I think, Miss Vyvyan, the only thing we can do is to prepare for it immediately as soon as we can."

" I see; everything is exactly as you say," replied Anna, " and now let me ask you a favor. I am stronger physically than you are, and I beg you to allow me to undertake the heavier share of our occupation. Let me do all that requires to be done outside the castle, such as getting wood and water, and whatever we may want from the wreckage, and you take charge of the inside of our present home, in which you must allow me to help you. I understand you already, and I believe you would do everything and endure all the fatigue without a murmur, but that is impossible; you have not the strength, and you must try to be well for the sake of your dear child."

Mrs. Carleton endeavored to remonstrate with Miss Vyvyan about the division of the toil, which was so new and strange to each of them, for she was born with a great generous heart that was ready and willing to do and die for others; but Anna would not listen to her sweet pleadings, although in her soul she admired them.

"Bow wow," said the little one, pointing down to the forest.

The ladies looked over the battlements and, to their horror, saw three wolves creeping stealthily along under the shadow of the great pines below. They thought instantly of the the fallen door at the entrance, and hastened down the tower stairs as far as the room hung with green velvet tapestry, where they had passed the night, and which they decided should in future be their sitting-room, so they named it the green parlor. As they entered, the glow of the cheerful fire on the hearth, the beautiful prospect of forest and sea from the windows, and the child's butterflies, glancing here and there, gave a bright and pleasant air to the room, but the ladies felt much disturbed by the discovery of wolves so near them, and the knowledge of the open door in the passage below.

"Miss Vyvyan," said Mrs. Carleton, "there are other doors of entrance to this castle; I saw

them, we will go and see if we can open one of
them ; and then we will close up the door below
altogether."

At the end of a passage leading from the tower,
and not far from the green parlor, they found a
massive door, strongly barred and bolted inside.
They drew the bolts, and on opening it led down
on the outside, by a long flight of stone stairs to
the grass below, and very near to the place on
which they stood on their arrival from the beach.

"We shall be safe in one respect now," said
Mrs. Carleton, "for no animal can break this door
and we can keep it bolted."

The first thing to be done now was to close up
the entrance down stairs. The ladies went down
and out through the door by which they had
entered the castle at the north end. Quickly
gathering up some of the wood which lay round
about them, they set fire to it, in order to scare
away any wolves which might be prowling near,
and at once went to work, carrying stones from
the ruins of the fallen tower, and by their joint
strength replacing the door. They next piled up
such a barrier of great stones behind it, that they
were sure that no wolves could enter that way.
They had finished their first attempt at building and
were about to go up again to the green parlor,
when the child with a little laugh and in its spright-
ly way cried out,

"Kitta, kitta, see kitta." At the same instant
running as fast as her tiny feet could go, after two
small white kittens which the next moment disap-

peared down the half-dark stairs, that they had
noticed when they first arrived, but were too tired
to investigate at that time.

They now looked down them and in the dim
light, saw only a passage which led in the direction
of the fallen tower. They satisfied themselves
that there was no opening from that to the outside
of the building, and concluded that the immense
pile of ruins completely stopped up all means of
ingress that way, so they decided not to go to the
bottom of the gloomy staircase for mere curiosity,
when time was so precious to them, for they felt
as Mrs. Carleton had remarked that winter might
be upon them very soon. They passed all the
remainder of the day in bringing up from the
beach such supplies as they most needed, and decided to devote a portion of each day to this occupation as long as the weather permitted.

Before sunset they were all safe in the castle
again, the child running about the room they were
arranging, and delighted with the many beautiful
ornaments. The ladies made up their minds to
adapt themselves to their circumstances, and be as
cheerful as they could, for the child's sake. They
selected the tower for their residence, as it contained the best rooms in the castle, and the view
from every one of them was beautiful. They
could go up the watch tower and look off from the
battlements, over the islands and forests, to those
majestic purple mountains, whenever they desired
to do so.

A sleeping room next to the green parlor was

chosen for Mrs. Carleton. It was fitted up with
the same degree of luxury as most of the others,
the furniture being of satin wood and ivory, and
the hangings and drapings of the bed and windows of pink velvet and white lace. Two curiously
wrought silver lamps stood on the dressing table,
and showed that they had burned themselves out.
In front of the mirror was a jewel casket ; it was
open, and showed rings and aigrettes of diamonds
and emeralds. A few ruby ornaments lay on the
table, and a string of pearls, also a small lace scarf
and a pair of lady's gloves, embroidered on the
backs with gold. The curtains and velvet draperies of the windows were completely closed, and
the room looked as though some one had dressed
in it and gone away and left the lamps burning.
Everything was a mystery to the ladies which they
could not unravel.

When the day was over, Mrs. Carleton and Miss
Vyvyan sat beside the sleeping child, in Mrs.
Carleton's room. The fire was burning on the
hearth, and the full moon poured its beams in at
the windows ; they had no other light.

Mrs. Carleton spoke much of her bereavement,
but struggled to be brave, and to resign herself to
a destiny she could not alter, at the same time
revealing, quite unawares to herself, a character
full of intense affection, unselfishness and great
courage.

As Anna watched the sweet, pure face so full
of emotion and sensibility, and the firelight flick-
ered upon and lit up the refined features, her whole

heart yearned toward her new friend, and her own sorrow was buried in those of the forlorn young mother.

"I have been considering," said Miss Vyvyan, "about your child. Do you not think we ought to make life as bright and happy as we can for her, and we can do a great deal, although we may have to stay in exile for a long while. She need never suffer from that idea. All will depend upon the way we educate her, and the way we live.

" Exactly so," replied Mrs. Carleton. "We will make our lives as good an example as possible ; we will bring her up, as far as circumstances will admit, the same as we would do if she were in my old home. We cannot have the servants we have been accustomed to have, but we can make this home a systematic one, and a refined one, and we must make it a cheerful one for her sake." There is one thing I feel very anxious about," said Mrs. Carleton ; "my child has not yet been baptized. As I told you, we were going to take her to England for that purpose. I should feel happier if I could carry out my husband's wish, and be able to call her by the name he so much liked."

" I can fully enter into your feelings," said Miss Vyvyan. "Why not baptize her yourself? I presume you are familiar with the service, as we have baptisms in our church so frequently."

" Yes," replied Mrs. Carleton, "and I cannot see that there would be anything wrong in doing so, myself, as there is not any one else to do it."

" It can no more be wrong," said Anna, " to

repeat the baptismal prayers for your child, than it is to offer up your daily prayers for her. Indeed to me it seems perfectly right, as we are situated at present."

"I am glad you entertain those feelings on the subject, Miss Vyvyan," replied Mrs. Carleton, "and as we are both of the English church, will you be godmother to my little one?"

"You confer great happiness on me," replied Anna, "by making such a request. What do you intend to call her?"

"Cora was the name my husband wished her to be called," replied Mrs. Carleton. "and I desire to add Caroline to it, as that is the name of my dear mother, and is now, alas, the only means I have of showing my affection for her, who is perhaps at this moment mourning my absence."

"Will you baptize her tomorrow?" inquired Miss Vyvyan. "If you will, we can make a dress for her in the forenoon. There is an abundance of white India muslin and cashmere, too, enough I should say to dress her for years to come."

"Yes," answered Mrs. Carleton, "I like that idea, and we will keep her always dressed in white."

"And as to yourself," said Anna, "I ask you as a favor, to let me choose for you in this instance, I wish you always to be beautifully dressed in colors, that will look bright and cheerful. I think it will have an influence on the child's spirits and thence on her health. I do not feel that we need to have any compunction about using the things we find here, for we see that this place must have

been deserted many years ago, and I cannot help
thinking that all these costly things are the plun-
der of buccaneers."

"Nothing is so probable," answered Mrs. Carleton. "Indeed, when we consider for a moment,
everthing seems to say so. Many of those cases
which still remain unopened are such as the merchants bring to the colony of Virginia. I have
seen similar ones there which came from foreign
countries. It occurs to me that all these stores
are the cargoes of ships that have been robbed by
those desperate men who have been and still are
the terror of the sea; but why they left this place
so suddenly is difficult to divine, unless, perhaps,
retribution fell upon them when they were out
at sea on some of their marauding expeditions.
Evidently a lady has lived here, too; perhaps they
took her with them on their last voyage, and she
also may have been lost, so I think we may feel
we are not doing wrong in using such things as are
necessary to our existence while we are here."

The next morning the ladies were up early
·busying themselves with their preparations for the
child's baptism. As they sat by the open window
in the green parlor, making the little white dress,
the sunlight falling upon the floor, the soft, warm
breeze from the south coming in upon them, and
the beautiful child playing about the room, prat-
tling to herself in her baby language, and trying
with her little hands to cover the colored shadows —
butterflies as she called them,— and to hold them in
one place, they each of them thought to them-

selves how much there is in life to make us happy;
and yet, and yet, who can be happy when there is
an empty place which nothing here can fill. They
neither of them expressed what they thought, for
they had each made a resolution to help the other.

The sea and sky were one beautiful blue; there
was just sufficient breeze to cause white caps at
distant intervals, and to toss the surf lightly
against the rocks.

The ladies finished their sewing, and with the
child went out to gather some wild flowers to
adorn their parlor for the baptism. In a few
minutes they saw a narrow path which they followed and found that it lead to a well of pure
water only a little way off. Below this was a
swamp surrounded by a luxuriant growth of asters
of every hue, and white and pink spirea and golden
rod, and blue iris, and the delicate, rose-colored
arethusa, and the blue fringed gentian abounded
on every hand; also shrubs of the bayberry,
wild rose and sweet brier, with many beautiful
ferns.

By Mrs. Carleton's refined taste the green parlor
was soon transformed into a fairy bower. The
autumn sunshine sent a flood of golden light over
all, and the child, dressed in its fresh white attire,
was baptized, and Miss Vyvyan was its godmother.
The ceremony was just over and the latter lady
was still standing with the child in her arms, beside
a large crystal bowl which was placed on the table
and embedded in green moss and wreathed round
the top with white roses. It contained the water

4

from which the child had received the symbol of
the Christian church.

"Now," said Mrs. Carleton, "I wish to say to
you, Miss Vyvyan, that from this day Cora belongs
to both of us, to you as well as to myself; she will
henceforth be *our* child. I want you to have someone you can speak of as 'mine.' I am thankful
that I never knew what it was to be without someone of my own to love, who was near to me, but I
can picture to myself what a death in life such an
existence must be to those who have to endure the
separation, and I should feel very selfish if I did
not divide my happiness with you."

"I do not know how to answer you," said Miss
Vyvyan. "I cannot say what I wish to. Will you
grant me one more kindness; that is, let Cora
always call me by my name, Anna, and you do the
same. It is more than three years since anyone
called me Anna; there is no one left to do so."

"I will," said Mrs. Carleton, "and to you I must
be Ada, for so I am named. I am glad that you
are pleased at having Cora for your godchild. I
thought you would be; that was a little plan of
mine. I wanted to do something to make you fee
happier."

Gentle, loving Ada, always thinking of the good
she could do to others, always self-abnegating, always giving up her own happiness that others
might receive pleasure; even in the midst of grief,
bereavement and exile, devising means to cheer a
life that she saw was more lonely than her own
—such was her character.

The position in which Miss Vyvyan now stood as Cora's godmother created a sincere bond of friendship between the two ladies, which as time went on developed into a lifelong affection. They each understood and appreciated every thought and feeling of the other. The child, who was of an intense and affectionate temperament, loved both of her guardians. She confided in Anna and would stay with her for hours together, and she always demanded in her baby way that Anna should partake equally with her mother and herself of everything that she deemed pleasure and enjoyment, and if Miss Vyvyan remained long out of sight, inquiry and desire were expressed by Cora in one little sentence, "Anna be back." At the same time, with an innate and delicate discrimination, the child defined the distinction between her filial love for her mother and that given to her friend in so natural a way that neither of the ladies could ever feel slighted or wounded in the least degree.

CHAPTER VIII.

He who ascends to mountain tops, shall find
The lofties peak most wrapped in clouds and snow;
He who surpasses or subdues mankind,
Must look down on the hate of those below.
Though high above the sun of glory glow,
And far beneath the earth and ocean spread,
Round him are icy rocks, and loudly blow
Contending tempests on his naked head,
And thus reward the toils which to those summits led.

THEY had been domiciled in the castle for several days when Miss Vyvyan said,

"As I am to take care of the commissariat department out of doors, Ada, I think it would be well for me to go down to the beach and bring up all the provisions I can, while we have such fine weather, as we think the winter may be very long here, so if you consider it a good plan I will fill another storeroom."

"We will all go down, Anna," replied Mrs. Carleton. "We have been here five days now, and I hope the tide may have removed much that was distressing to see there."

When the ladies reached the beach it was as Mrs. Carleton had supposed, all the corpses had floated away, but the whole beach and the shore far up from the sea was still strewn with wreckage. They worked very diligently, making piles of many things that might be useful, little Cora trotting about as busily as her companions, and helping as far as she knew how. It was scarcely ten o'clock,

but the ladies had been out in the sun for some
time lifting and carrying heavy burdens, an occupation which was as fatiguing to them as it was
novel. So that they might rest a little while, and
get all the sea breeze that there was on that still
day, they went out on to a mass of high rocks,
which projected into the ocean and formed a cove
on each side.

Scarcely had they seated themselves, when they
saw a gentleman climbing up from one of the
coves below and coming toward them. He was a
young man perhaps twenty-seven years of age.
As he approached them, they noticed that his
appearance was that of a gentleman of rank, his
every movement was full of grace and high breeding, his figure was slender and under the middle
size, and his face exceedingly handsome and refined. His bright chestnut colored hair was long
and fell in waving masses on his shoulders. He
wore a small beard of the same hue, his dress was
very rich and elaborate, after the fashion of the
time, and when he spoke, his voice and courtly
manner, told that he was what his appearance
indicated. As soon as he came near to them, he
bowed low, and made a gesture with one hand, as
if raising his hat, but he was bareheaded.

"Ladies," he began, "pardon me for intruding
upon you, but for the love of heaven give me a
cup of water, it is many days since I moistened
my lips, I have been shipwrecked on your coast."

The ladies were on their feet in an instant. Mrs.
Carleton running to a birch tree a few yards back

from the beach, and breaking off a piece of bark, deftly bent it into a cup, which she handed to Miss Vyvyan to fill from the same pond that had sup- plied them with water the first day they were thrown upon the island. Refreshed by the draught the stranger tried to thank them, but speech and strength failed him, and tottering a few paces toward the land, he fell down insensible beside a fissure in one of the rocks. The ladies went to him.

"His hands are as cold as if he were dead, Ada," said Miss Vyvyan. "What will it be best to do?"

"What did you do for me, when you first tried to help me?" replied Mrs. Carleton.

"I tried to get you warm."

"Well, then, we must do that."

At these words, they simultaneously took off the outside wraps they wore, and laid them over him, and hastened about among the wreckage, until they had a good supply of warm rugs and cover- erings.

"Where did you get those hot stones that you placed at my feet," said Mrs. Carleton?

"I made a fire and heated them."

Then we will make a fire and do the same thing.

They covered the poor fellow over, and put hot stones to his feet, and he seemed to be sleeping. In the meantime they prepareed some light food for him. They sat in silence near by, waiting to see what they could do, should he return to con- sciousness. They observed the color coming back to his face, and a bright pink spot burned on each cheek.

" I fear, said Mrs. Carleton, fever is setting in."
" I will make something with the fruit we brought down, that will quench his thirst."

The child seemed to echo the thoughts of her companions, seeing them anxiously engaged in ministering to the sufferer. She began gathering up anything that she thought pretty, and laid it by his side. Presently she went to him with a few wild flowers, which she had picked from the crevices of the rocks and among the shore grass close by. She observed the ladies spoke in low tones to each other and moved about very quietly. She knew there was some cause for this, for, young as she was, she had already an idea of illness and suffering, and her little heart was full of pity for others. She stood looking at him as he lay asleep before her, waiting with her wild flowers, until the time should come for her to give them to him. " Poorest, poorest," she repeated, at the same time stroking his hair with her baby hand. That was her own word, and her own way of showing sympathy and pity. The little one's vocabulary was, at this period of her life, very limited, but equally significant of all that she saw and felt. She possessed no extraneous babble. The only words she was capable of uttering came from her heart ; hence they fell upon her hearers with all the beauty and strength of truth. "Poorest, poorest," she again repeated; "dorn seep ; papa dorn seep, too."

At the child's last sentence, a shudder quivered

through Mrs. Carleton's frame, and a still whiter shade passed over the already pale face. · She clasped her little one close to her and bowed down upon its head. She did not utter a sound. Her silence said more than any words could have done, for hers was a sorrow that had no speech.

After a restful sleep, the young man awoke, and sitting up among the many rugs and coverings by which he was surrounded, he looked about in every direction, and appeared to be endeavoring to realize his true position. He saw the high tower of the castle rising so near to him among the trees ; he saw the ladies and the child, but he did not feel quite; sure of the truth of all he saw until Mrs. Carleton put a cup into his hand and said,

" This is a fever drink ; will you take some ? I have just made it from fruit, the same as we make it in Virginia."

" Thank you," he said. " I know what it is. I am a Virginian. I sailed from that colony in the ship Sir Walter Raleigh. Who has been so kind as to bring me all these rugs," he continued.

" We did," replied Mrs. Carleton, looking in the direction of Miss Vyvyan, who with the child stood near them.

" What, with your own hands ? I regret to have caused you so much trouble ; although I am grateful to you in the extreme, I would have preferred you to have given orders to some of your servants. It is not seemly that ladies such you are should wait upon me ; it is not consistent with the chivalry of a gentleman."

"I understand your feelings on this subject," said Mrs. Carleton, "for I, too, am a Virginian ; but we have no servants now, and my friend and I are glad that we can be useful. It is five days since your ship was wrecked, therefore we know that you must have suffered greatly. Pray do not be disturbed by seeing us doing what little we can to save you from perishing ; let me assure you that we are very happy to do our utmost."

The young man bowed, his cheeks still wore the bright flush of fever which heightened the inten-sity of his soft brown eyes, that beamed with grati-tude.

"Do you say that you are a Virginian ?" he in-quired, addressing Mrs. Carleton.

"Yes," she answered ; "we were in the Sir Walter Raleigh, too ; that is to say, my husband and child with myself, but I never saw any of the passengers. I remained in my cabin all the time we were at sea."

"I recollect you, now," he said. "I saw Colonel Carleton lift you and your child into a boat when our ship went ashore."

"Were you acquainted with Colonel Carleton?" she inquired. "He was my husband."

"We were not acquainted until we met on board, but during the several weeks we were at sea we passed all the time together. You say he *was* your husband. Is it possible that generous-hearted man is lost ?"

Mrs. Carleton made an inclination with her head.

4*

"Forgive me," he said, "my conversation has caused you pain."

"Please continue," she replied, "tell me all you know about him."

"I witnessed many of his acts of kindness during our voyage, and received kindness from him at what I suppose was the last moment of his life. The boat you were in was full and I urged him to get into another one, but he refused, saying, 'I can swim and you cannot.' At the same moment he took hold of me and dropped me into the boat as easily as if I were a child. You know how tall and powerful he was. The next instant your boat was capsized and I saw Colonel Carleton leap into the sea and swim toward you. His hand was almost upon your arm, when an enormous wave swept him out of sight. The same wave capsized our boat, and the next one threw me into the cove below. I might have got away before, but part of a broken mast lay across my chest and I was entangled hand and foot by the rigging. I could neither move nor call aloud. I heard voices more than once, the voices of ladies. I believe it was your voice and that of your friend, for I never knew my ear to deceive me. I saw corpses lying all around me. The tide took them away and brought them back again many times while I was there. All one night a dead hand lay across my throat, but I could not disengage my hands to remove it. I had no fever; I was conscious of everything. The tide was higher than usual this morning. It lifted the mast and I crawled from under it."

He appeared to suffer much from exhaustion and lay down again upon the rugs, and closing his eyes remained silent. After a little rest, he again sat up and resumed his conversation with Mrs. Carleton.

"I have a great love of music," he began. "I left the colony of Virginia with the intention of going to London, to perfect my study of that divine art, under the direction of Orlando Gibbons. He is very young to be a composer, but he is already of much renown."

For some time he continued to speak fluently on the subject of music, a subject of which the ladies perceived he was a complete master. As he talked, he became full of enthusiasm, and that wondrous light which belongs to genius alone illumined his beautiful eyes and his whole soul spoke through them.

"Ah, my madrigals," said he, "they will yet be sung to His Majesty, King James. My symphonies I shall submit to Orlando Gibbons, then I shall hear them played by a full orchestra, the world will hear, then justice will be accorded to me, the great masters will be my judges, genius such as theirs allows them to be generous and true in their opinions of other men. They will see me as I am. They will not condemn what they cannot understand. They will not call my life useless, because my tastes, my talents and my whole being compel me to be different from those among whom I live. I cannot help it, and I would not if I could."

An expression of mental pain passed over his

face as he thus proceeded. "Why did my uncle
call my life and my work useless? It is hard to
be misunderstood. If I can create out of my own
brain something that is pure and beautiful, that.
gives happiness, that draws coarse natures away
from their coarseness, to feelings more elevated,
that can bring to some an ecstacy of delight, to
others a sweet calm. If I follow a pursuit which
injures no human being, no living creature, why
am I to endure displeasure? Is it more manly,
more noble to hunt the poor, panting deer till it
falls gasping on the ground, and then to save it's
life for the purpose of chasing it again for sport?
Is it more noble to ride races till the horses drop
down dead? Tell me, do such pursuits elevate or
brutalize?"

Taking a roll of paper from his breast, he handed
it to Mrs. Carleton, saying, "I have a symphony
here which I composed since I left my home;
would you like to look at it? I wish my twin
brother Ronald could see this; he understands me,
and he will understand my music, although since
his accident, his hand can no longer obey his will;
yet he will read my symphony, aye, more, he will
play it in his soul. With it you will find a song
also, the words and music are both mine; when
you have read it, will you hand it to your friend?"

Mrs. Carleton took the roll of music into her
hand, but observing that the writing was almost
obliterated from having been so long wet with sea
water, she passed it to Miss Vyvyan, who sat a
little farther off, desiring to spare him the pain of

seeing that his composition was destroyed. The many pages of music were entirely illegible, with the exception of part of the refrain of the song, the words of which ran thus : —

> Bury me deep,
> Where the surges sweep,
> And the heaving billows moan.

At the bottom was the name "Ralph." The following part of the signature was destroyed.

As Anna read over the words of the song, she could not help feeling that they might be prophetic of what was very near. She folded the paper together and returned it to him.

" Is that your signature ?" she asked.

" Yes, that is my name," he replied. " Do you like music," he continued.

" I do," she said.

" How much do you like it ? "

" I like it to such a degree," she replied, " that I think life is not life without music."

" Ah, that is what I think," he said. " But I am exhausted. Ladies, will you pardon me if I sleep a little while? I want to get back my strength, that I may be able to wait upon you both, and make all the return in my power for your great kindness to me."

He soon fell into a restless, broken sleep, constantly murmuring to himself incoherently.

" Anna," said Mrs. Carleton, " he is very ill, and it is almost sunset, and quite impossible for us to take him up to the castle. We must make some shelter here for him ; the breeze already comes in from the sea much cooler, and the night will be cold. The ladies picked up loose stones and planks and everything they could move, and formed a low wall around him, making a place of shelter as large as a small room. They then drew up a portion of a sail and laid it partially across for a roof. He still slept, but as they looked at him, they saw the fever was rapidly increasing; a still brighter flush was on his cheeks; his lips were parched, and his breathing distressingly short and oppressed.

"What can we do?" said Mrs. Carleton. "See there, Anna! The sun has gone behind the hill to the west of the castle; it will soon be dark. It would be terrible to leave him here to perish, for he needs great care, beside the wolves may come, and he is too ill to defend himself. Do tell me what you think it best to do?"

"One of us must watch by him to-night, Ada," replied Miss Vyvyan, "and if he should be better to-morrow, we may be able to get him up to the castle. I must be the one to watch. Little Cora could not pass the night without you, and even if she could, you are not well enough yet to be out in the night air. Let me go up and get a few things such as he may require. I will be back very quickly."

When Miss Vyvyan entered the castle, the sun had set, and a dull gray hue had settled upon every room. How dreary for poor Ada, she thought to herself, here almost alone, with the death of her husband so recent, and so vividly brought before her to-day. She at once thought of kindling a fire as the only means she had of taking away some of the gloominess of the place. She did so, and then spread a supper table as temptingly as she could with the only food they had at command, and hastened back again to the beach.

"He still sleeps," said Mrs. Carleton, "but his fever is very high. It distresses me to leave you here, Anna, and I would not, but for little Cora's sake."

"I understand you" replied Anna; "I shall always understand you. We are not mistresses of our own destiny; we have to do what we can, not what we wish. I know all that you would do if you could."

As Mrs. Carleton took the child in her arms and turned her steps toward the castle, the moon rose slowly from the sea and made a long, golden, glimmering path from the horizon to the shore. It was the harvest moon, which was almost at the full. The night was light and still, with the exception of the sound of the waves, which broke upon the beach below in one long, continuous moan.

Anna watched beside her charge, sometimes moistening his parched lips, sometimes arranging his improvised pillow, and listening to every sound both near and distant, with that quick, discriminating sense of hearing which we acquire from watching over those we love, and which she had learned during the last illness of her mother. The night was now far advanced. Close beside her came the quick, hard breathing, and the indistinct murmuring of the sufferer.

From down below, still arose the mournful tones of the heavily rolling waves, and from the forest came the howling of the wolves, but she could hear they were not near; and resolved if they should approach to scare them away, by setting light to a pile of wood which Mrs. Carleton had laid together for that purpose.

As she sat there on the ground and realized her situation, a feeling almost of terror came over her. During the past few years, she had gone through the discipline of a long lifetime. This night, the past and present seemed to combine to crush out the remnant of courage that had been left to her. She buried her face in her hands androcked to and fro, struggling with her feeling, struggling with destiny, and struggling to call back some of her former self; that as her day, so her strength might be.

At that moment, Ralph awoke; he turned his face on his pillow, and regarding her with great earnestness, he said, "Where is Ronald, my brother? I want him here now."

Anna went nearer to him and, looking at the flushed face and the brilliant, restless eyes, saw that he was delirious.

"Ronald," he repeated. "Are you there?"

"Perhaps he is near you," said Anna, wishing to solace him.

"That is well," he answered. "I will play my new composition to him."

He immediately began to move his hands over the rugs which covered him, as if he were playing the organ.

"Ah," said he, "that is the chord I sought,—
thank heaven. — Listen to this,.— Hark, hear this
resolution. Now do you see what that chord leads
up to ?—How is that harmonic progression ?—How
does this sound ? — I shall have a double suspen-
sion there. — Ah, that is good.— Hark ; now can
you hear the melody running through the minor ?
— Yes, the violoncellos come in there, — so it must
be.— More ink ; quick, quick,— there is so much
to write and so little time."

He sank down again, exhausted, and fell into a
deep sleep. After an hour he again awoke, the
flush had left his cheek ; he was very calm, and
had perfectly regained his senses.

"I have been dreaming of my brother Ronald,"
he said. "I thought he was here. Can you tell
me what time it is ? "

"I think," replied Anna, "by the position of
the moon, it must be an hour past midnight."

"I have been ill," he said, "but I feel better,
much better ; almost well again. I want to thank
you ladies for so much kind care of me ; both Mrs.
Carleton and you, but I do not know what to call
you. I did not hear your name."

"I do not wish you to thank me now," said
Anna, "because you are too weak to talk at pres-
ent, but I will tell you my name. It is Anna
Vyvyan."

"Vyvyan," he repeated. "I know that name ;
I will tell you all about it to-morrow — I feel faint.
—There is a great oppression at my heart.—Those

timbers crushed my chest. — I cannot breathe. — Raise me up."

Anna knelt on the ground beside him and raised him up as he desired.

"Yes," he said, "tired, tired."

The next moment a wonderful far-away look of rapture came over his beautiful face, and then a pale shadow such as might be caused by the passing flight of a bird ; — his head fell upon her shoulder ; — he was dead. Anna laid his lifeless body gently down and watched beside it through the silent hours of the night, gazing from time to time at the finely-formed features. They had a fascination for her, and she could not dispossess her mind of the thought that she had seen them before.

The first few streaks of dawn came creeping over land and sea, and the sun arose and shed a shimmering light on the surrounding islands, the forest and the misty mountain tops. With daylight, the howling of the wolves ceased, and the only signs of life were the sea gulls that floated about near the shore or ran screaming along the beach devouring their prey, and a pair of eagles which constantly hovered near and swooped down close to where the dead man was lying. Anna covered the cold, pale face and went nearer to protect it from any attack.

The sun had not long risen when Mrs. Carleton with little Cora left the castle.

Anna heard their voices, and went to meet them. " I must be careful how I speak," she said, addressing Mrs. Carleton, "for I feel sure Cora understands much more than she can find language to express, but I have to tell you that ever since about an hour after midnight I have been all alone. He sleeps."

The ladies gave the child some shells to play with, and went to where his body lay. They drew the sail over the low wall which they had made around him and completely covered in the little room.

"That will keep any eagles or wolves away while daylight lasts," said Mrs. Carleton, "but we must bury the poor fellow's body before night. The thought of having it devoured or mutilated when it is in our power to prevent it, is more than either of us could bear, for in addition to the forlorn state that we found him in, his genius and his gentle breeding made both of us take an interest in him. Beside, his being a Virginian, and the last person to speak with Dudley, gave him a claim on my friendship."

They went up to the castle and did not return until just before sunset, when they brought with them many beautiful wild flowers, which, as we have said, abounded on the island. They also gathered branches of the fragrant fir balsam, with which they lined the fissure in the rock on which Ralph's body was lying. Folding around the latter a robe of rich brocade, they lowered it tenderly into the tomb that nature had wrought. As Anna laid the face cloth over the marble features, she started back. The resemblance which had attracted and held her attention during the night, had come out vividly since the morning. The likeness was to her own mother, and was as marked as if Ralph had been her son. They covered his silken winding-sheet with flowers until the sepulchre was filled, then they laid flat stones across his resting place, and began to build a cairn over all. They continued building until the sun went down, little Cora bringing stones in her baby hands and placing them with the same precision that she saw her mother and Miss Vyvyan were doing.

"We have made everything secure now, Anna," said Mrs. Carleton, "but we will come again to-morrow and add more stones to the cairn, and every time we come to the beach we will do the same. Will you take charge of the manuscript? We do not know what the future may bring. He wished his brother Ronald to see it, and we may, perhaps, some day have it in our power to carry out his wish. Now we will go back to the castle, for I see you are in great need of rest."

CHAPTER IX.

Disdain and scorn ride sparkling in her eyes,
Misprising what they look on
.   .   .   .   .   to her
All matter else seems weak; she cannot love,
Nor take no shape nor project of affection,
She is so self-endeared.

HE maple leaves had turned from rose and crimson to orange, then to pale yellow and to brown, and had fallen to the earth, for it was now almost Christmas, but no snow was as yet on the ground. The ladies had made all the rooms which they occupied in the tower very comfortable and homelike, although they could neither of them bring themselves to speak of the place by the name of home, for that was a sacred word to both of them. They always spoke of their dwelling-place as the castle. We have already said that the views from every room in the tower were of exceeding loveliness. Most of the windows overlooked the islands, many of which were far away, others perhaps only two or three miles off. At one time, their beauty would be softened and half obscured by mist, at another they would appear to be lifted up into the sky by the effect of the mirage. At times a heavy sea fog hung over the island and obscured every distant object, and to the nearer ones gave a weird and spectral look.

Just at daylight one morning, when the fog was coming in from the ocean, the ladies were awakened by the lowing of cattle. On looking down from the tower windows, they saw some cows come out from under the trees and pass along close to the walls of the building. They scarcely had time to express their surprise to each other, before it was much heightened by the appearance of a woman, who followed the animals out of the forest and drove them quickly across the grass which had formerly been the courtyard of the castle, to a high mound a little way to the north of it, there both she and the cattle disappeared in the fog and among a thick growth of spruces. The woman's movements were quick and firm, and she stepped as one who not only possessed determination, but defiance also. She was tall and guant and bony, possibly not fifty years old, but her hair which hung loose in disheveled entanglement, was as white as if she were eighty. She had large black eyes that flashed upon every object that she looked at. She wore a red dress, which reached only a little below her knees. On her feet she had a pair of heavy, high boots, such as are worn by cavalry soldiers. Her head was partially covered by an old cotton handkerchief which had once been of many bright colors.

"Did you hear what language she spoke," said Miss Vyvyan ?

"I caught the sound of a few words somewhat like Italian, but it was not Italian."

"I heard it," replied Mrs. Carleton. "I believe

it was Spanish, but she passed so quickly I could not hear distinctly, or I should have understood her."

All that day the ladies remained in doors. They watched in the direction of the mound, but nothing was to be seen which would lead them to suppose that any dwelling was near to them ; and so the time passed until night covered the island with darkness. They had put little Cora to bed, and were, according to their usual habit, sitting beside her in Mrs. Carleton's room. The night was unusually cold. It seemed as if winter had really sent in its heralds in advance, to announce its near approach. The wind howled and shrieked through the rooms which surrounded them up stairs, and groaned and roared in the many passages and apartments down below. Their glowing log fire was so acceptable to them, that they were loth to leave it, and so they sat talking together until midnight. They had gained a very good idea of time by observing the sun and moon, and were also greatly aided by the ebb and flow of the tide. They knew exactly the high-water mark, by certain rocks ; they knew that it took so many hours to ebb and so many to flow, and they had become so familiar with the sound of the outgoing and incoming tide, that even in the darkness of night, they did not feel at a loss.

" "It is past midnight, Anna," said Mrs. Carleton, going to one of the windows and leaning out to listen, "The tide has just turned. Come here," she continued. "What is that rising above the mound ? "

"Sparks of fire and wood smoke," replied Miss Vyvyan. "There must be a dwelling of some kind there. That is probably where the woman went to with the cows, but it is strange that we have never seen anything of it before to-night.

The intense cold of the next day warned the ladies that they must use dispatch in finishing their arrangements, in order to be able to meet the exigencies that a severe winter night might bring upon them. During the two months they had been living in the castle, they had employed them-selves continually in bringing in supplies of all kinds, until they felt they had ample stores to last them for a very long time, but they were all in the rooms down stairs ; and as the distance from the tower was so great, and the weather so severe, they decided to make a storeroom up stairs, on the same floor as that on which they lived. They had been busy for some time, packing and carrying up their requirements, little Cora, as usual, just as active as themselves, taking up her loads and returning for more ; her tiny feet pattering up and down the long, stone staircase, flitting back and forth between her mother and Anna, with her own peculiar, light, swift, graceful movement, which was like that of a bird.

All at once, they each missed the return of the child ; but as the ladies were in separate parts of the castle, they each of them thought she had re-mained with the other. After some time had elapsed, they began to feel anxious, and each sought the other.

Meeting on the stairs, the question "Where is Cora?" came from the lips of each of them at the same moment; then a hurried explanation, and a terrible feeling of horror. They ran in every direction, calling her name. They separated and went different ways; they met again and went in search of her together. Could it be possible that she had gone up the watch tower, and fallen from the battlements. They flew up the tower stairs and looked over. They rushed down again and out into the court yard; no sound, no sign of the child. In the agony of their distress, they went into every room and opened every great chest, every large piece of furniture.

"Oh Anna," cried Mrs. Carleton, "that woman we saw, do you think she has stolen my child; perhaps put her to death. We must go to the mound where we saw her go."

They followed the tracks of the cattle, and pushed their way through the trees for a short distance, till they came to the almost bare mound; it was high and long; near the base was an opening of irregular shape, which was evidently the entrance, but it was partly closed by an old, broken door. They had gone within a few feet of it, when the door was violently thrown down, and the gaunt woman in the same strange dress stood in the doorway, brandishing a rusty sword at them, and speaking rapidly in a peculiarly harsh and high pitched voice. She spoke in Spanish, which Mrs.

5

Carleton perfectly understood, and which she, also, spoke fluently.

"Go hence," said the woman. "What seek you here? I am Louisita, and all that you see here is mine; my land, my trees, my seashore; hence I say, away with you, or this sword pierces the heart of both."

"Pray, hear me one moment," pleaded Mrs. Carleton, "I am in the greatest distress."

What care I for your distress, have I not enough of my own without listening to yours? Off with you."

"Only a few words," again entreated Mrs. Carleton. "I want to — "

"You may want, I heed that not. I want myself; I have nothing to give you. I would not give you anything, if I had it. You are intruders on this island. I saw you arrive, and the men you brought with you. Ha! ha! You meant them to land here. Where are they now? I saw it all, ha! ha! ha! You may wait for their return; they have made a long voyage, so long that they will never come back; glad, glad, I hate the accursed sex, they caused all my suffering; twenty years entombed here, through their state of mad intoxi. cation. If only one of that great band of pirates had remained sober, I might have got away."

"Do let me ask you, have you seen my child?" said Mrs. Carleton. "I entreat you to tell me."

"See your child. I saw you take food to one of the accursed sex. I saw you try to make him live. I despise you for it. Why should he live to drink,

drink, and bring misery on me and all women ? I
tell you again I hate them for their love of drink.
I hold them in contempt for their weakness. The
ocean did well to swallow them down, just as their
brothers swallowed down the fiery drink on that
fearful night when the great tower fell and crushed a
hundred of them."

"Do, I implore you, say if my child strayed anywhere in your sight ?" cried Mrs. Carleton, over-
come with anguish. "We have lost her."

"Lost her; lost her; seen her;" echoed Louisita
very slowly, and making a long pause as if to col-
lect her thoughts, she added, "The child was
young and the wolf was hungry."

As Mrs. Carleton translated the last sentence to
Miss Vyvyan, she fell fainting into Anna's arms.

"Do not heed what she says, dear Ada; let us
believe the best until we know the worst. Cora
may have fallen asleep in some of the nooks in
the building, and so did not hear us call her."

The ladies returned to the castle. Miss Vyvyan
was also under the most intense apprehension, but
she concealed her feelings from Mrs. Carleton.

"Which room were you in, Ada, when you
missed Cora ? She may, as I said, be asleep, and
perhaps she is among some of the bales in one of
the storerooms."

"I was down at the end of the passage," replied
Mrs. Carleton, "in the largest room. We will go
there first."

They went down and searched the room, but
could not find Cora. As they came out of it they

heard a sound which seemed to come from under
ground. They ran to the half-dark stairway which
they had seen when they blocked up the north
door. The sound was more distinct; it was Cora's
voice in conversation. Who could have taken her
down to that subterranean place? They did not
hesitate an instant, but descended the stairs as
quickly as the darkness would admit, and found
themselves in a dungeon where there was just sufficient light to see that an uncovered well was
close beside the path which they were following.
The talking had ceased. The silence was profound and added still greater gloom to the place.
They both stood bending over the well and looking
down into the depth of water which was black and
silent. They each looked at the other. They read
the thoughts which passed through each other's
mind. They neither of them spoke. They did
not dare to. While they still stood bending over
the well, straining both eyes and ears to the utmost, little Cora's voice came again. It seemed
close to them; they could not distinguish any
words, but the tones were those of her usual pretty
baby prattle. Was that voice from the spirit land?
They could see nothing but the gray stone walls
of the dungeon, the dark, open well and some large,
loose stones, which had heavy iron chains with
rings attached to them, and which had in former
years been fastened to the ankles of the prisoners
and worn by them till death relieved them of their
burden. Just in the same way as many of the poor
victims of imperial tyranny are to-day doomed to

drag their chains and weights while they labor in the mines of Siberia. 'Again came Cora's voice as if from the further corner of the dungeon. The ladies stumbled among the loose stones in the semi-darkness, Anna, who was more robust and the taller of the two, folding her arms around Mrs. Carleton to support her, and both of them feeling their way lest they should fall into any other well or excavation. Arrived at the corner they saw a gleam of light, which came in a slanting direction through a large hole in the wall. They still heard the little voice and determined to follow it. The hole would only admit of their crawling in on their hands and knees. This they did for several yards, until everything was in complete darkness, and they found they were against a wall straight in front of them, and could go no further. The passage was too narrow for them to turn round and come out, the top of it was so low it nearly touched their heads as they crawled along. The air was oppressive, and suffocation almost overpowered them, but they could still hear the voice which seemed nearer. Feeling the walls carefully with their hands, they found that a sharp turn to the right, led along in a direct line toward the sound. This passage was also dark, and as narrow almost as a coffin. They continued crawling for several yards more, sometime cutting their arms with the broken stones which covered the bottom, and sometimes placing one of their hands upon some cold substance which moved and felt as if it might be a lizard or a sleeping snake. They neither called nor spoke, for they feared someone might have the child, who would run away with her, if warned of their approach, so they determined to come upon them suddenly. They were greatly exhausted, but they struggled on.

At length daylight appeared at the end of the subterranean passage, and in another moment they emerged from it and stood in a large stone hall, amply lighted from above by open iron gratings and loopholes in the walls; through one of the latter, a bright gleam of light fell like a halo upon the sweet, fair face and the golden head of the child, who was sitting on the floor, with a portion of her little white dress folded around a kitten, which she was rocking in her arms and talking to. Happy as was her wont and all unconscious of the flight of time and the anxiety that she had caused, she seemed to have made some little exploration of her own since she had been there and wanted to show her discovery, just the same as Mrs. Carleton and Miss Vyvyan were always doing to one another.

"Come," said she, getting up from the floor and taking her mother's hand, "funny sing down dare; Anna too," she continued, and stretching out her other hand, she caught hold of the folds of Miss Vyvyan's dress, and drew her along also, leading them both across the hall to a large gate of iron bars. It was locked, and closed the entrance to a broad stone passage.

"Down dare, funny sing," she went on, pointing to a skeleton, which lay just inside, and so near to

the gate that one hand had been thrust out between
the bars and the bones of it were lying close to
their feet. A great quantity of long black hair
still remained about the skull, in the midst of
which was a Mexican ear-ring of elaborate workmanship. Everything told them that the skeleton
was that of a woman. Glancing round the hall,
the ladies could not see any door. How did Cora
get there? Before they had time to inquire, little
Cora saw something inside the gate, and with her
usual quick movement, she swiftly passed her tiny
hand between the closely placed iron bars and from
a small heap of débris of finger bones, drew out a
richly chased gold ring, inscribed with the name
of "Inez;" set in it was a large ruby in the form
of a heart.

The child who possessed as part of her inheritance a fine, sensitive instinct, looking at her
mother, observed that her long silken eyelashes
were wet with tears, and that traces of recent
mental agony lingered on her face. In an instant,
the dear little soul strove to comfort and cheer,
after the manner so often employed by each of her
guardians toward herself. Holding up the ring
in one hand, and clinging round her mother with
the other, she said,

"See, mama, Cora. dot pitty sing for mama.
Don't ky, don't ky, Cora loves mama."

"Sweet child," exclaimed Anna, taking her up
into her arms and holding her to her heart. "Sweet
child, more precious to us every day, for each one
reveals some new beauty of character, some still

more lovable trait. Come, dear Ada, come away,"
she continued. "I will carry Cora. How did my
little godchild come here?" she said, addressing
the little one in her arms.

"Kitta doe," answered Cora.

"Yes darling, where did kitta go?"

"By dare," said the child, pointing to a massive
column, one side of which was built close to the
wall and had the appearance of being placed there
as a support, but was in reality to conceal a doorway which led to a flight of stairs between two
walls.

The ladies went up, Miss Vyvyan carrying Cora.
They soon found themselves in one of the rooms
which was nearly filled with firearms and other
implements of warfare. The entrance to it at the
top of the stairs was concealed in the same manner as the doorway below, and but for Cora following the little white kitten, the ladies might have
lived many years in the castle and never have seen
it. The subterranean passage into which they
accidentally crawled, had been made for a place of
concealment in case of a sudden attack upon the
castle.

CHAPTER X.

Like the leaves of the forest when summer is green,
That host with their banners at sunset was seen: ·
Like the leaves of the forest when autumn hath blown,
That host on the morrow lay withered and strown.

For the Angel of Death spread his wings on the blast,
And breathed in the face of the foe as he passed;
And the eyes of the sleepers waxed deadly and chill,
And their hearts but once heaved and forever grew still.

.   .   .   .

And the idols are broke in the temple of Baal;
And the might of the Gentile unsmote by the sword,
Hath melted like snow in the glance of the Lord!

CHRISTMAS had come and gone, and the snow was lying deep on the ground. They had seen nothing of Louisita since the day Cora was lost.

"I wonder," said Mrs. Carleton, "how that poor woman, Louisita, exists? for I think from what I saw the day we went to her, that she is all alone, and if you recollect, she said something to that effect. I fear she suffers in this cold weather. You saw, of course, that it was no kind of a house that she came out of."

"Yes," replied Miss Vyvyan, "it appeared to be only a mound of earth.

"I want to take her some food," continued Mrs. Carleton. "Do you think we can get there through the snow?"

5*

"I can carry Cora," replied Miss Vyvyan, "if you can take the food."

Mrs. Carleton filled a box with both food and fruit, and the ladies, with little Cora, went forth to visit Louisita.

She met them in the same manner as before, not allowing them to come very near to the opening, and brandishing the old sword.

"If that child were one of the accursed sex," she said, with a malicious look, "I would sever its head from its body."

The child could not, of course, understand her language, but she read the look, and clasping her arms closely around Anna's neck, she buried her face on her shoulder.

"Will you accept of this?" said Mrs. Carleton, speaking very gently, and at the same time lifting the lid of the box.

Louisita sprang at the contents as a famished tigress might have sprung upon some long-sought prey. Jerking the box out of Mrs. Carleton's hands, she put it on the ground, and again raised her sword. "Hence," she cried, "all of you; no one enters here. Ha, what do I see; stop, stop," she screamed. "Donna Inez, my lady, Donna Inez. Where did you get that ring," she continued, pointing to Mrs. Carleton's finger, on which she wore the ring that Cora had found. "That is the ring Donna Inez wore the night they murdered her. Yes, the accursed sex murdered her, the night they drank out of the skulls till they were all mad, mad, and the great tower fell upon them ; ha, ha, ha. Who will drink out of their skulls when they find them? More of the accursed sex, they who make laws to command women, and who cannot command themselves. Away with you. I tell you to go, you are intruders."

"I fear your dress is not warm enough," said Mrs. Carleton. "You must suffer from the cold."

"Suffer," shrieked Louisita, "I have known nothing else than suffering for twenty winters and summers, and they the accursed sex caused it all by their passion for the fiery cup; it soddened their brains ; it poisoned every good feeling in their hearts. It buried my husband under the ruins of the tower; it bereft me of my home; it caused my two babes to die of cold and hunger in this tomb."

"Poor Louisita," said Mrs. Carleton, "if you will come back with us to the castle I will find some warm dresses and other comforts for you."

"Never," she replied ; "it is haunted. I have not been into it since I came away with my babes the morning after the tower fell."

"Why do you think it is haunted?" asked Mrs. Carleton.

"I know it is because I hear them shrieking in the night, and I hear Donna Inez calling, "Open the gate."

"I will not ask you to come inside, Louisita, but if you will only come up the outside steps to the door I will get you anything you wish for."

"I want food; I want warm clothes; I want something to cover my bed."

"You shall have it," said Mrs. Carleton. "I feel very sorry for you; I wish to make you happy."

"Ha! ha! happy," she repeated. Then looking toward Miss Vyvyan she continued, "Make her take that child out of my sight. She brings it here to mock me. I will run my sword through her heart if ever she brings that child here again."

"She does not bring my child here to mock you, Louisita. She is my friend, and loves my child, and we could not leave it alone. My friend always goes where I go, for fear anything might befall me. She cannot speak Spanish or she would explain all to you."

"Go away with you," said Louisita; "go get the things for me. I will come for them when I am ready, but I will not put my foot over the door sill."

"All things considered, Ada," said Miss Vyvyan, "I think it is well that Louisita is afraid to go into the castle, for she appears to be of a spiteful nature, and might try to do Cora some harm, but we will never again let the child be out of sight."

Mrs. Carleton prepared for Louisita's arrival by placing a number of things of all kinds in the hall near to the entrance which the ladies used. In a little while she came, still in the same short red gown and cavalry boots, bearing the old sword in her hand.

"Where are my things?" she demanded of Mrs. Carleton, speaking in the same defiant tone as usual. "Bring them here to the door. I told you

I would not enter. That belonged to Donna Inez,"
she said, taking up a dress, "and that was Don
Alphonzo's," seizing hold of the red velvet cloak
which the ladies had found in the library.

"Wrap the cloak about your shoulders, Louisita," said Mrs. Carleton; "it will keep you warm."

"I will not," she answered, fiercely; "it belonged
to one of the accursed sex; he died through drink-
ing of the fiery cup; he caused the death of many
through the same thing."

"Perhaps you will wear this, Louisita," said Mrs.
Carleton, offering her one of the best and warmest
table covers that she and Miss Vyvyan had brought
from the wreck.

"Yes," said she, "I will;" give me another for
my bed."

"Let me go, Ada," said Miss Vyvyan, who had
hitherto been standing far back in the hall with
Cora. "I know where we put one that will please
her, for I see that she likes red," and taking Cora
up in her arms she disappeared.

"Why does she take that child everywhere,"
asked Louisita.

"I told you just now," replied Mrs. Carleton,
"that my friend loves my child, and they are
always happy together."

"Does she think she is happy?" said Louisita,
"what a fool she must be; she is not happy, you
are not happy, I am not happy. Oh, the fool, she
has not sense enough to know that she is not
happy."

Just at this junction Miss Vyvyan returned with

Cora on one arm, and the other one loaded with warm, bright-colored articles, such as she felt sure Louisita would like. As she approached the door, where the woman stood, and passed the things to Mrs. Carleton, the child again clung tightly as before to Anna, who hastily went back to the end of the hall.

"Tell the fool to go away out of my sight with that child," said Louisita, "and I will tell you about this place. I will not tell her because she mocks me by bringing the child to remind me of my dead babes—my babes who were famished to death."

Miss Vyvyan went to the green parlor with little Cora, and Louisita began her narrative.

"I was born in Spain. When I was a young woman, Donna Inez was married to Don Alphonzo in Madrid. She engaged me for her waiting woman. I was married directly after to one of Don Alphonzo's sailors. We came to this island in one of the Don's ships. The castle was most gorgeously furnished with the spoils of almost every country in the world. I thought Don Alphonzo was a great noble, so did my husband, for he was so called in Spain, but soon my husband told me that the Don and all his men were buccaneers. Donna Inez did not know the truth until after we came here. We tried to get away, but that was impossible. The Don brought the richest dresses and jewels to make the Donna like her home, but he could not succeed. Many wrecks I have seen in just the same place you were wrecked

in ; Don Alphonzo and his crew burned false signals
at night, they hoisted false colors by day, they
drew the unfortunate ships to their doom ; the Don
had a hundred men in this castle, ready to obey
his commands at any moment. They had uniforms
and flags of many nations, which they used as
disguises and decoys. They robbed the vessels
which fell into their hands, they killed some of
their crews, some they sold into slavery, and others
who refused to commit murder, they chained to
·great stones down in the middle dungeon. That
was called the 'dungeon of death,' for they kept
the men there until they died of starvation, and
when they died, they threw their bodies into the
well. My husband, Juan, was put into that
dungeon, because he would not kill a Spanish boy
who was taken prisoner, but Donna Inez made the
Don release him, for we thought Juan would help
us to get away. The Donna had promised to give
him half of her jewels, if he would find some way
to get us back to Spain, but he made himself powerless, he soddened his brain, he murdered his
manly feelings ; he was once good and brave and I
loved him with all the intensity and devotion of a
true woman, but he learned to value strong drink
more than my affection, he killed my love, he
drowned'it in the fiery cup, and I grew to despise
and loath·him. Don Alphonzo was worse than
Juan, for he had so much learning and so much
power and he turned it all to a bad use. He
blasted other lives by his own evil example. Out

of his wickedness grew the curse which fell upon me, but he has met with retribution."

"Poor Louisita," said Mrs. Carleton, speaking very gently, "What can I do for you?"

"Nothing," she replied. "Let me tell you the rest. One night the Don and his crew came back with the greatest prize they ever seized. The men were summoned to unload the ship. They made immense fires from the castle to the beach, and by their glare they robbed the merchants of their valuable cargo. It was near midnight before. their rapacity was satisfied. Don Alphonzo ordered the vessel to remain where she laid until daybreak, when he intended to set her adrift, with all her crew on board, that he might see them dashed on to those rocks which you see down yonder. The Don then commanded a feast to be set in the banqueting hall, in the base of the north tower. He ordered every man in the castle to attend the revel, that they might rejoice over their great prize. They all went; the wine flowed like water; they went down to the banqueting hall by a secret stairway; they passed along a stone passage, which was closed by an iron gate. The banqueting hall had no windows; they always held their revels there, that they might not be surprised by any enemy, for no light could be seen outside, and no one could tell that they were carousing. . I listened on the secret stairs until their loud shouting had ceased, and I knew that the strong drink had soddened their brains, and paralyzed their arms. I ran to Donna Inez; I dressed her in the richest

brocade ; I covered her neck and arms with jewels
of fabulous worth, for I knew the effect of costly
attire upon the accursed sex whose help we needed.
I made ready some caskets of jewels to take with
us. I told the Donna all that I had heard of the
ship lying there till morning, and we resolved to
let the captain know that the Don and all his men
were powerless, and to offer him the Donna's jewels if he would take us away. We knew he would
be glad to escape ; we knew he would be glad of
the jewels, for they would make him very rich.
We were ready to leave the castle. My babes
were very young ; they were asleep in a large
basket ; I could easily carry them to the beach.
We heard a sound like a moan ; it seemed far off,
then a distant rumble, but nearer than the first
sound ; next a terrific roar ; another and a fearful
crash, crash. For a moment the whole castle
trembled ; a flash of light lit up the place ; the
north tower was wrecked from top to bottom ;
the walls fell inward ; they fell as you see them
lying now, for no hand has touched them since.
We knew an earthquake had occurred. My babes
awoke and screamed ; I tried to quiet them, and to
hold Donna Inez back, but she tore herself away ;
she was panic stricken ; she did not know what
she did ; she said something to me as she ran out
of her room about seeking protection ; she rushed
down the stairs in the direction of the banqueting
hall ; she never came up them again. As soon as
I had hushed my babes I followed her. She was
inside the iron gate ; it had closed upon her as she

passed through. It could only be opened by those
who understood the secret spring. There was no
one who could come to show us how to open it.
We could not break the gate; that was impossible.
We saw that the further end of the castle was
stopped, all filled up with immense blocks of stone
which had crashed in when the tower fell. Don
Alphonzo and more than a hundred men lay under
the ruins; they shrieked and groaned there all
through the night. Donna Inez became frantic.
She dashed herself against the iron bars like some
newly caged bird. In the morning when the sun
came up from the sea she was dead. I looked for
the ship; it had sailed. I had almost lost the
power of moving, but the cries of my babes called
me back to activity. I gathered some covering
and some other things and took them to the Vikings' tomb. I tore away the earth to make an
entrance. We lived there till cold and hunger
killed my babes. I have lived there ever since.
Nothing could induce me ever to enter the castle
again."

"Why do you call it the Vikings' tomb, Louisita?" asked Mrs. Carleton.

"That was what Don Alphonzo called it. I
think he knew for he was a man of much learning,
although he had no sense. He said the Vikings
built the castle very long ago, and lived here for
two hundred years till a great pestilence prevailed
among them, and so many died of it that the remaining ones deserted the place. He said the
Indians cast a spell over the Vikings and bewitched

them, because the Indians used to live here in wigwams before the Vikings came and drove them away from their own land, and would not allow them to bury their dead among their forefathers, for they have a burial place on this island. It is down there just below the swamp where I saw you gathering flowers one day soon after you came here. There is a large elm tree down there, the only one near. The Indians are buried there all round it. They always had an elm tree in that place. They have a secret charm by which they keep it there. The Vikings cut down their. elm many times, but it sprung up again in the night, and was as tall and large as ever the next day. When we came here Don Alphonzo had their tree cut down every day, but it always came up again just the same. At last he was afraid the Indian spirits would cast a·spell over him, too, so he let their elm alone. The Indians still bury their dead under it, but no one ever sees them arrive. They come in the night. An elm will always grow there till the two thousand years for which they have their charm has expired. After that time there will never be another."

CHAPTER XI.

A fool, a fool!—I met a fool i' the forest.

HE first winter which the ladies and little Cora passed on the island, was unusually severe, but they had expected and prepared for it ; and the winter scene was so novel to them, and fraught with so much beauty, that they never wearied of it. Besides the constant occupation in their housekeeping and attending to Cora, and also caring for Louisita, and providing her with all the comforts they had in their power to take to her, for she still insisted in living in the Vikings' tomb, which she never permitted them to enter.

Spring came at last, and with it returned to the island the robins, the song thrushes, the beautiful golden orioles, and the humming birds, all of which had gone southward at the beginning of winter. The wood violets and the trailing arbutus blossomed among the grass. The spruces and pines put forth their young buds, and the whole island wore a garb of beauty.

The little family of three, spent much time out of doors, and visited the beach almost daily, for they all loved the sea, especially little Cora ; and to enhance her happiness was the first desire of of both of the ladies. They frequently wandered around Ralph's grave, and never omitted adding a stone to the cairn, which they had raised to his memory. Little Cora with her tiny hands, always placing her own mite to the pile. As the child grew stronger, they took longer walks, and taught her from the book of nature as they went along, for Nature's lessons in geology, and botany, and natural history, lay all around them.

They had by this, brought their lives into the same degree of system and order, as that in which they had each of them been educated in their respective homes; the want of which during the first part of their residence on the island they greatly missed. They now divided their days, and had regular hours for certain occupations, and they made a compact, that they would always be cheerful in the presence of the child, and meet their destiny bravely, that they might not give a somber tinge to her young life. Everything went well with them as far as might be, excepting that Louisita, who had the control over three cows, would never let them have a drop of milk for Cora. The child had for a long while after their coming, constantly repeated at every meal " Dinah, bing milk." She seemed to think her negress nurse was somewhere near her, and was able to bring anything she wished for, as formerly.

Her demands for milk, had ceased for a week or two, when one morning she again begged for it, and when told she could not have any, a look of extreme repression of feeling came over her features. She did not cry, or in any way show temper. The food was distasteful to the poor little

thing ; and the look of forced endurance, one may
say that forced resignation and endurance combined, which we sometimes see in older faces
and which is utterly discordant with their reas.
oning faculties, was distressing to behold in one so
young. The child could not understand why she
was not to have milk ; but the brave spirit of her
mother was her birthright, and like her mother,
she endured disappointment without a murmur.

"This must not be any longer, Ada," said Miss
Vyvyan. "It is too much for you to witness, and
for Cora to suffer. That dear child shall have
some milk. I will learn how, and I will milk one
of those cows, whether Louisita's sword kills me
or not."

"Dear Anna," said Mrs. Carleton, "I pray you
do not expose yourself to danger ; do not be rash.
Why what has come to you? I never heard you
speak like that before."

"I know it, Ada, but you never saw me so placed
else you would have. I detest selfishness, and you
have been so kind to Louisita, and she is aware
how precious Cora is to us. You know we shall
not be depriving her of anything, because she told
us she threw most of the milk away ; but she en-
courages the cows to come here in order to keep
them tame. You recollect that she told you the
rest of the herd which stay on the other side of
the island have become wild."

"I, of course, know that we should not be depriving Louisita," said Mrs. Carleton ; 'but I fear
so much that she may hurt you,"

"Only teach me a few words of Spanish, Ada," said Miss Vyvyan, "and I will put that out of her power. Teach me to say I am a spirit, you cannot harm me."

"I am afraid, Anna; for your own sake I would not have you go."

"I am not in the least afraid of her," replied Miss Vyvyan. "I have always done my best to help her, and I certainly intend to continue to be kind to her, because she needs help; but I never submit to injustice being done either to my friends or to myself. I consider it unjust to throw away the milk which Cora so much requires."

With those words Miss Vyvyan left the room. In a few minutes she returned.

"Ada," said she, addressing Mrs. Carleton, "my good old guardian, Sir Thomas, used to say 'All is fair in love and in war.' Now I am going to unite both love and war, for as I love you and Cora I must in all honor defend you both, just as some gallant knight would do if he were here. Put your hand on my shoulder and feel what is there."

Mrs. Carleton did so.

"Why, what have you under your dress?" said she.

"A whole suit of chain armor, Ada, that's all, and a helmet of the same under this lace scarf on .my head. Louisita won't have the pleasure of piercing my heart this time, and when she finds that she cannot, she will think the spirits are round me, or that I am like the Indians and have a charm. I am going now; the cows are in sight,

I saw how Louisita milked, and I think I can do it.
Look down from the window, Ada, and see the
fun."

"Anna be back," said the child, looking up with
a face more full of anxious desire than inquiry.

"Yes, precious one," replied Miss Vyvyan,
"Anna will come back."

No sooner had Miss Vyvyan approached the
cow and was endeavoring to imitate as well as she
could Louisita's way of milking, than the latter
came striding out of the mound wearing her cavalry boots and flourishing her sword, exclaiming,
as usual:

"Hence; away, away; all here is mine. Touch
not that cow. I will pierce your heart."

Miss Vyvyan who heard it all did not take any
notice of her, but went on with apparent indiffer-
ence, pursuing her lacteal occupation. Louisita
stood over her and went through all the sword
exercises that she was mistress of. Still Miss
Vyvyan continued her endeavor to milk, unharmed
either by cut or thrust. Presently, turning to
Louisita, she repeated her Spanish lesson as well
as she could in the midst of her laughter.

"It is the fool who is laughing," said Louisita,
looking up at Mrs. Carleton, who was leaning out
of one of the tower windows. "It is the fool, who
has not sense enough to know that she is not
happy. I shall never interfere with her again ; she
can have all the milk she wishes for ; she has a
charmed life."

CHAPTER XII.

The quality of mercy is not strained;
It droppeth as the gentle rain from heaven,
Upon the place beneath. It is twice bless'd.
It blesseth him that gives and him that takes.
'Tis mightiest in the mightiest.

UMMERS and winters went by ; five years had passed since the family had been cast on the island; they had watched from the tower almost daily for a white sail, but none had ever appeared, and yet they always continued to hope that the day would come, and they struggled within themselves to be patient and cheerful. Sometimes the thought would take possession of the mind of each of the ladies, that one or other of them might die, and how terrible it would be for the one who was left, and worse still a thousand times, both of them might die and leave Cora ; but neither of them would ever breathe a word which could convey such an idea to the other ; and when such thoughts and feelings oppressed them, they took the best method of dispelling their anxiety by engaging themselves in some active occupation. They made a pretty garden for summer enjoyment out of doors, and another for winter in one of the large rooms, by filling boxes and chests with earth. They always had beautiful flowers in their parlor, which was a

6

great source of delight to Cora, as well as to
her guardians. The two guitars which they had
found in the castle, they strung with wire, and
managed to have some music every evening in
the twilight; then they had a time set apart,
also in the early part of the evening, which they
called Cora's hour. For that period, they devoted
themselves wholly to the recital of such subjects
as were suitable and pleasant to her, and which
they varied every day in the week, weaving
each recital into a little story, sometimes telling
from history; at another time, Mrs. Carleton
would compose a story about Virginian life,
and Miss Vyvyan would tell one about foreign
countries; but the hour Cora liked best, was the
one devoted to poetry and fairy tales. She was
now in her eighth year, and could read very well;
but there were no fairy tales among the numerous
books in the library, so the ladies repeated them
from memory. When the friends had put Cora to
bed, they always remained together during the
rest of the evening, working, and reading aloud to
each other, making new dresses for Cora, who
grew very fast, or planning some pleasant surprise
for her, and as far as their present position allowed,
always considering the child's future, and in what
manner it was their duty to educate her, so that
she might be best prepared to encounter any of
the reverses or changes of condition, which fate
brings into the lives of so many of us.

Louisita had taught the ladies how to poison
some of the provisions with a plant which grew in

the woods, and by so doing, and laying the poisoned food about the ground, they had destroyed nearly all the wolves, and now wandered about the island where they desired, making expeditions in search of flowers, or having little picnics for Cora in the woods, and visiting Ralph's cairn without their former fear. They had all been spending a long summer afternoon on the beach, the ladies seated on the rocks between Ralph's cairn and the sea, Mrs. Carleton working on a dress, that she was making for Louisita, Miss Vyvyan reading aloud, and Cora filling in the small open spaces in the cairn, with little stones of her own selecting. The sun had gone behind the the hill on the western side of the castle, when the little party left Ralph's cairn and strolled along the shore, as they returned homeward, gathering the beautiful sea-pea blossoms on their way.

"Anna," said Mrs. Carleton, "we have not seen Louisita to-day; shall we go to the mound and tell her that her dress will be finished in the morning, perhaps that would please her?"

"I am ready," replied Miss Vyvyan, "to go anywhere you please, Ada; you always know the right thing to do."

"May I stay a little way off with Anna," said Cora, "not far; I am afraid of Louisita, but I want to be near you, mama, to take care of you. Don't you think, Anna, that Louisita is very cross," said the child.

"Not now, dear, she has been very gentle and quiet for the last year."

"I remember," the child continued, "a long time ago when I was little and you were trying to get some milk for me, and she hit you with her sword, she frightened me so ; I was afraid she would kill you."

"She does not carry her sword any longer," said Miss Vyvyan, and she does not scold us any more ; she would not hurt any one now, your mama has been so kind to her, and set her such an example of goodness that she has made her good, too."

They had reached the entrance to the mound ; Cora shrank back and clasped Miss Vyvyan's hand, who led her a few steps on one side.   •

"What is this," said the child holding in her hand a gold ornament set with garnets that she had just picked up from a heap of rubbish which appeared to be sweepings from Louisita's abode.

"That is a fibula, Cora, such as I saw in a museum in Norway."

"Look, Anna, look at these" she continued, gathering up several antique beads of glass mosaic and a few chess men of amber from the same place. "Tell me what they are ?"   ·

"They all came from Norway," replied Miss Vyvyan, explaining their use to her.

Mrs. Carleton meanwhile knocked on the broken planks which served for a floor, and as Louisita did not appear she entered the mound, but soon came out again, and whispered something to Miss Vyvyan who passed in, leaving Mrs. Carleton with Cora. On first entering, it was difficult to distinguish the interior of the place, or any of the numerous objects that it contained, as the only light came in through the shattered door, and a small hole on one side of the mound, which evidently served as a chimney and a window also. After a few seconds, when Miss Vyvyan's eyes became accustomed to the extremely subdued light, she saw that she was in a place that was four or five hundred feet in circumference and about twenty-four feet high. Advancing toward the side on which the hole was broken, she observed Louisita. A gleam of light fell upon her. She was kneeling in front of a small structure which formed a table. Her hands were clasped in the attitude of prayer, and her fixed and glassy eyes seemed to look up in the direction of a small silver crucifix, which hung on the wall before her. Her features were set and rigid. The rich brown Spanish tint had left her face. When Miss Vyvyan looked upon her she knew that she was dead, and, on laying her hand upon her cold brow, she concluded that death had taken place many hours previously; perhaps the night before. She summoned Mrs. Carleton, and bidding Cora sit down where they could see her from the inside of the mound, the ladies proceeded to lay Louisita to rest in the same tomb that had so long been her dwelling. They lifted her on to her bed ; they folded the poor, tired hands of the weary woman, whose life had lingered on through those lonely, loveless years. They took the silver cruci-fix from the wall and laid it upon her breast ; for although they were not of her creed, they respected her devotion. They felt thankful that in her life-

time they had done all they could to lighten her
burden. They felt still more thankful for her own
sake, that her pilgrimage was ended, and that she
had gone to join the babes who were so dear to
her mother's heart.

Not finding sufficient boards to close up the
entrance securely, the ladies went to the further
end of the place to get some which they saw there.
The pile was very high, and as soon as they took
hold of one, several other boards fell in broken
pieces at their feet, revealing the ribs of an old
Norwegian ship, inside of which lay the skeleton
of a man which had been there so long, that it
began to crumble to ashes the moment it was exposed to the air. They turned to leave the ship
when another and much larger fall of boards
exposed the skeleton of a horse. They paused a
moment and looked round ; they saw that Louisita was not in error when she had told them that
the Norsemen were at one time on the island, for
there was every evidence of the mound being the
tomb of a Viking. Among the bones of the horse
lay the remains of a bridle and saddle of leather
and wood, the mountings of which were in bronze
and silver. Near that of the man lay some ring-
armor, a shield-buckle, two stones of a hand-mill
for grinding corn, bits for bridles, stirrups, some
gold finger rings and a fibula of the same metal.
The ladies passed quietly out of the tomb, and
built up the entrance as well as they could with
stones and earth, across which they drew the vines
and brambles that grew among the spruces close

by, so that at the end of the following summer
there was not any trace left of an entrance ever
having been there.

. . . .

Mrs. Carleton had missed Miss Vyvyan for a
longer period of time than usual one day, and in
going in search of her to a part of the castle which
they rarely went into, she found her engaged in
making a little gift to surprise Cora with, and singing in a low tone the following song : —

WHY?

Oh weary years why come and go
   With endless sorrow rife;
And hope's dead dreams why come ye back
   To mock my empty life?

Oh destiny, oh bitter fate,
   Oh burning tears that start,
Why must the hearts that love the most
   Forever dwell apart?

Mrs. Carleton entered the room so gently that
Miss Vyvyan was not aware of her presence until
the former was close beside her.

"You look sad, dear Anna; what can I do to
cheer you?"

"This is a sad anniversary for me," replied Miss
Vyvyan; "but I did not intend you to know it."

"Let us hope, Anna, that time will give us back
some of our former happiness," said Mrs. Carleton.

"The grave is unrelenting, Ada; it never gives
back what it has taken from us. I will tell you all
some day. I cannot talk about the past now; it
would unfit me for being of use to others who

have suffered; it would make me no companion for you and dear Cora; it would be selfish to intrude my life upon you."

"No, Anna, pray tell me why I sometimes see so sad an expression on your face which you change the instant you find I am looking at you. You know you have never alluded to any event in your life prior to our being shipwrecked. You have told me of your childhood, certainly, but that was so bright and happy that the recollection of it must be an endless source of thankfulness. Now I again pray of you, tell me all."

"As you so much wish it, Ada," replied Miss Vyvyan, "I will tell you that the sunlight went out of my life too soon. At the time I first met you the world was all darkness to me; all my days and years were winter, and my only wish was to die."

"Oh Anna, do not say that," said Mrs. Carleton; "but go on and tell me why."

"Forgive me, I fear I was rebellious, but I only thought of the present. I could not look forward; it seemed as if there were no future for me here. I was alone; the only lips which had the right to breathe my name were sealed in death, and the stately dignity or cold respect with which I was always addressed reminded me hourly of my isolated existence. I have no words that can express to you the utter desolation I felt in having no one to call me by name. I often sought the whispering of the wind through the trees, the leaves and the long, waving grass in the hope that it might emit a sound which my fancy could fashion into the once familiar name, but all in vain ; the trees and the leaves and the grass, even the rocks and hills, whispered and murmured and talked of many things, but the sound I most longed to hear came never."

Anna noticed that Mrs. Carleton looked sorrowful. She ceased speaking.

" Why did you stop, Anna ; go on."

"I am distressing you, I see," answered Miss Vyvyan ; "I ought not to pain. you."

" Please go on, Anna."

" I cannot expect you to comprehend my exceeding loneliness at that time, because your life has never been empty, and you have now your beautiful child. When first I met you I had nothing. When I say nothing, I do not mean to infer that I was destitute of worldly means. I had an ample fortune which I inherited from my mother, besides the manor house and the landed estates of my grandfather ; but I was destitute in the deepest sense ; I had nothing of my own to love ; I was alone. Do you know what that word alone means, ' when hope and the dreams of hope lie dead ?' No, Ada, you cannot, God grant you never may. At length there dawned that rich, golden autumn day, when you named Cora, and gave me the right to say ' My.' The surprise was so great to me that I scarcely knew whether I was moving about in a dream, for my existence had been so long void of interest that I deemed happiness for me dead. But when I took Cora in my

6*

arms, and looked into the wondrous eyes, and saw the love, the purity and the delicate sensibility of the being to whom I could always in the future say 'My,' a new world and a new existence seemed before me, and I thought angel voices thus whispered and said, ' We have brought this beautiful child into your life to dwell forever as a sweet, fair flower in the garden of your heart.' And as the child grew and talked and called me by my name, the music of its voice and footstep gladened my soul and sent a thrill of joy through my whole being. Ever since the day of our shipwreck, when you were lying on the beach so near death that I did not dare to allow myself to believe that you could live, (and may I say it, Ada, without seeming vain), when I was made the instrument to call you back to life. Ever since that day until this, you and Cora have seemed to belong to me ; to be mine to love and live for. So you see you have brought back the sunshine into my life. I have finished ; I shall never again talk in this way. My study shall be to brighten, not to sadden, the path which lies before you in the future."

Anna Vyvyan kept her promise to the end.

CHAPTER XIII.

The heart that has been mourning
O'er vanished dreams of love,
Shall see them all returning,
Like Noah's faithful dove.
And hope shall launch her blessed bark
On sorrow's darkening sea.

I have had joy and sorrow; I have proved
What lips could give; have loved and been beloved;
    I am sick and heart-sore,
    And weary, let me sleep;
    But deep, deep,
    Never to awaken more !

IT was September again, and the golden rod and fall asters, that had for seven seasons been Cora's delight, were once more in their yellow and purple glory. The day was sunny, and the rich autumnal glow spread itself over the walls of the old castle, the forest, the rocks, and the sea, and the island and its surroundings seemed to the little family to be more beautiful than ever.

Mrs. Carleton was engaged in decorating the green parlor with flowers and trailing plants, which Miss Vyvyan and Cora had gathered for that purpose. The two latter had gone down among the trees near the beach to get the last basketful of moss to complete the work of adornment.

"Quick, Trefethen, quick, hand me my gun ; see

those birds, what an immense flight of them," shouted a strong masculine voice within a few yards of the trees which concealed them from view, and which also prevented them from seeing from whom the voice came.

" Don't fire," cried Miss Vyvyan, instantly catching up Cora in her arms as she used to do in the child's baby days.

"Don't fire," she repeated, "there are people here who are coming out of the woods on that side," at the same time, forcing her way among the trees, in the direction from which the voice came; and taking the advantage of making an inspection without being seen herself.

Cora caught sight of two figures standing on the open ground between the forest and the sea.

She clasped Miss Vyvyan's neck more tightly and whispered softly, " Look, Anna, there are two papas."

Miss Vyvyan paused, and looking between the branches she saw a tall, finely grown gentleman in the full military uniform of a colonel of the British army. By his side stood a man of smaller stature who wore the blue coat of a sea captain of that period. As the sunlight fell upon the bright scarlet uniform, the gold laced hat, the gold epaulets and the handsome scabbard which contained the colonel's sword, the child gazed in great amazement, not unmixed with admiration.

As we have already said, Cora was born brave, and like her mother struggled to keep up a calm courage through any emergency ; but the poor little heart trembled a little when she said,

"Anna, I think he is a very pretty papa, but why does he wear that sword ? Louisita used to wear a sword," she added.

"We are safe, Cora ; he will not hurt us. He wears the uniform of our king. He would help us if we wanted him to."

"Shall we go to him ? " said the child.

"Yes; we must so that we can tell your mama what sort of persons are on the island."

A few more steps took them out of the wood. Miss Vyvyan put the child out of her arms and led her. The gentleman in uniform advanced to meet them, and raising his hat said,

"Pray pardon me if I caused you any alarm. I did not know that this island was inhabited, and I saw so much wild fowl that the temptation to shoot was very strong."

"I can quite understand that," replied Miss Vyvyan. "We need no apology," she added, "as we were aware that most gentlemen enjoy sport, and your bearing and the uniform that you wear assure us that there is no cause for alarm."

The officer bowed low, but made no reply.

Cora, who was still holding Miss Vyvyan's hand, looked up at her and said again, "What a pretty papa, and more papas coming from the ship; but I like this one best."

The child's excitement was so great that her whisper was very audible to the officer.

"What does she mean ? " he asked.

"That is her own way of expressing herself,"
Miss Vyvyan answered. "She calls all pictures of
men papas. We think she has some recollection
of her father, although she was little else than a
babe when he was drowned here, which is seven
years ago to-day. She appears in some mysterious
way to realize that there was such a relationship,
for she delights in looking at pictures of papas as
she calls them, more especially such as are represented as wearing military uniform. And when
she was very young I have often seen her press
her cheek against that of a small statuette which
we have of a soldier and kiss it and call it papa."

· While Miss Vyvyan and the officer were still
speaking Cora was examining the handsome uniform, and the gentleman was looking intently at
the gold chain that the child wore round her
throat. After a little conversation the officer
addressing Miss Vyvyan said,

"I hope you will not think me too inquisitive if
I ask whether this fair sea flower has a mother
living."

"Oh yes," cried the child before Miss Vyvyan
had time to reply, "I have the dearest mama in
the world and we do love her so, don't we Anna?"

Cora in her enthusiasm let go Miss Vyvyan's
hand, and taking hold of the officer's,

"Come," she said, "come with us and see her,
and then you will love her, too."

Miss Vyvyan was about to suggest that proba-
the strange gentleman would prefer not to accept
Cora's invitation until he had received one from

her mother, when he' interposed by asking Cora what her mother's name was.

"Why, it is mama," she replied.

"Yes, fair one; but she has another name."

"Oh, you mean Ada, that is what Anna calls her."

"She is Mrs. Carleton," said Miss Vyvyan.

"Great Heaven! my prayer is answered," exclaimed the officer. Turning quickly away for a few paces he covered his face with his hands, and his stalwart frame trembled with emotion.

"What is the matter," said Cora, "are you unhappy; never mind, do not be sorry, papa."

"Yes, my beloved child, I am indeed your own papa who has come back to you and mama; take me to her; I must go to her this moment, show me the nearest way."

Cora again clasped her hand round one of his fingers and as she lead him along she said, " Mama will be so happy for she thought you could never come back to us, and she often told me that if we were good we should go to you some day ; poorest mama, big tears come into her eyes when she tells me about my papa."

Arriving at the end of the corridor leading to the green parlor Cora ran swiftly in advance of Miss Vyvyan and Colonel Carleton calling as she went,

"Mama, mama, we have found a real papa, not a picture, but my own papa."

Then came the meeting of the long-parted hearts and the recounting of events, which had

taken place since the day on which destiny had
torn the husband and wife from each other. Cora
full of fresh young life joined in the conversation
every instant, telling her father how they used to
get the eggs of the sea birds and the honey from
the wild bees' nest, and how they caught the sea
perch from off the rocks, and how she found a jar
of gold coins near the Vikings' tomb, which her
mama said were pesos, and all about the fibula
which she found there, also.

Then Colonel Carleton explained how he tried
to rescue his wife and child, just as Ralph had told
them a few days after they were wrecked; and
how he was picked up by a young man from Wales
who came out in the English ship, and was lashed
to a floating mast by that brave young fellow, and
by him kept from drowning until they fell in with
a slave ship that was bound for the coast of Africa,
but was also out of its course as well as their own
unfortunate vessels; and how they were taken on
board and kept toiling under an African sun for
nearly seven years, when good fortune smiled upon
them and they were sold as slaves and sent to the
colony of Virginia.

"The same young Welshman," continued Colonel
Carleton, has always been with me. He has a
very remarkable talent for navigation, and is now
the captain of my ship. If he had not been I do
not think I should ever have been able to find you,
for I did not know that it was an island upon which
we were shipwrecked; but he did, and under Providence, I have everything to thank him for."

"Beg pardon," said a voice at this part of Colonel's Carleton's narrative, and turning their eyes in the direction of the door they saw standing there the muscular, well-knit figure, the pleasant face and bright eyes of Captain Trefethen.

"Beg pardon," he repeated, "but I heard what the Colonel said about me, and I want to say, that if he had not cut off the leather belt he wore and let all his gold fall into the ocean, that I might have the leather to chew when I was famishing with hunger on the mast, I must have died; and I feel that under Providence I have everything to thank him for. I made up my mind then never to leave the Colonel till I saw him moored in a safe harbor. In a few days," Captain Trefethen continued, "everything will be ready for the good ship 'Ada' to sail for Virginia, and as I do not suppose the Colonel will want to take another voyage of discovery, I will leave you all there, as I intended to come back to these parts myself and settle on an island about forty miles down this bay. It has a queer Indian name, 'Monhegan' they call it. Captain John Smith, who is now ranging this coast, told me about it. He seems to have a fancy for Indian names. I shall never forget how he sung the praises of an Indian girl the night before he set out on his present voyage. 'Pocahontas,' he called her. Here is some fruit and a few little things for the ladies," he continued, placing a box upon one of the tables and leaving the room.

When Colonel Carleton was again left with his wife and child and Miss Vyvyan, he resumed his conversation, and answered all the anxious and rapid inquiries of Mrs. Carleton. " Yes," he said, " I assure you again that I left all the family in Virginia perfectly well. Your father attended to my estates during my absence, and by his wisdom in managing them, he has increased their value sevenfold. Your sister Julia was married two years ago, and she has an excellent husband."

" Excellent husband," echoed Cora, "What kind of thing is that? Mama and Anna never told me about the excellent. Where do you find it, is it a bird ; can it sing ; may I have one?"

Cora was about to propound further questions regarding an excellent husband when the merry peals of laughter from the two ladies and the Colonel, put an end to her interrogations. She did not understand why they all laughed, and like many of her elders under similar circumstances she felt sensitive on that account ; but with her usual quickness of thought, she said, " I know why you are so merry, papa ; it is because you are so glad to be with us all in this parlor, that mama has made so pretty with these bouquets and wreaths of flowers. Mama makes all our rooms pretty ; you ought to see them when the days are dark and foggy, so that we cannot see anything outside ; then mama gets so many branches of the fragrant fir and green moss and red berries, and makes the most beautiful things."

"Why does mama select the foggy days to adorn the rooms most, my darling?" said the Colonel.

"Why, don't you know? she does it to make Anna and me happy. Sunshine within, mama calls it, and Anna made a song about that; shall I sing it to you?"

Without waiting for a reply, the child sung the song all through, keeping time on her father's arm, which encircled her as she sat on his knee.

When the refrain "our sunshine is within" ended, Colonel Carleton bent down and pressed his lips upon the golden head of his little daughter.

There was a mist before his eyes as he said, "Yes, my darling, our sunshine is within our own hearts, and it is in mine to-day for which I thank God."

Cora continued talking, telling her father all about the beautiful flowers on the island, and the picnics on the sea beach and in the woods,

"And one day, papa," said she, "we went for a long walk to the north end of this island, mama said it was, and we saw such a pretty little island all covered with trees, and the eagles were up on the tall pines. It was so close to our island that we could almost jump on to it, and mama said I could think of a name for it, so I named it "Fairy island." I think our island that we live on is very pretty, too, but I am glad we are going to Virginia to live near grandpa and grandma and Aunt Julia and my uncles, and I want to see grandpa's dog Franco. Do you know, papa, I never saw a dog. And Anna must come, too, and live with us."

"Of course she will," said Colonel and Mrs. Carleton, both speaking at the same time; and per-

haps, added Cora, when it is summer, we will go
to England and visit Anna in her old home at the
manor house.

"That is right, Cora," said Miss Vyvyan; "the
way in which you have arranged for the happiness
of all of us is admirable."

"Yes," said Colonel Carleton, "Cora has made
a very pleasant sounding plan, but I am not as
sure as my little daughter appears to be, that we
shall be able to carry out the whole of it, for when
we land in Virginia, Miss Vyvyan, your cousin,
Ronald Fairfax, may have something to say in the
matter. From what Ada has already told me, you
seem to have felt great interest in poor Ralph, and
he and Ronald so much resembled each other in
all respects that it was almost impossible to distinguish them. Pardon me, if I say that I sincerely
hope you may take an interest in Ronald; besides
the affection that existed between these two brothers was so profound that Ronald will desire to
show his gratitude to you for your kind care of one
so dear to him. How is he to do it? I only see
one way."

The next few days passed by very quickly, as
every one was busily engaged in making their
preparations for the voyage. Full of autumn
beauty, the last day arrived, and the boat with its
crew waited on the beach for the family from the
castle.

"Oh dear," said Cora, who was standing in the
green parlor all ready to start, with her arms full
of her favorite golden rod and fall asters, "how

could I forget to pick up some of those shells which I like so much ; I wanted to take some to give to all of them at home, I am so sorry."

"There will still be time enough to get some before we embark, Cora ; you shall have some, dear," said Miss Vyvyan.

"Why Anna," said Mrs. Carleton, you are surely not going down to the breakers to-day ; I fear you will wear your life out for Cora's sake."

"Never mind me, Ada," replied Miss Vyvyan. "If I die in a labor of love it will be the death I most desire."

So saying she took a little basket and left the room. As she passed through the door Cora threw her a kiss and said, "Anna be back."

As we have said previously, the ladies liked Cora to keep some of her baby language, and that was one of her own modes of expression which they never corrected. It reminded them of her infancy and of their own mutual attachment, which first met in the love they each of them bore toward the child.

"Are you all ready ? " said Colonel Carleton, as he came along the corridor to the green parlor. "Where is Miss Vyvyan ? " he added, on entering the room.

"She has gone down to the breakers to get some shells that Cora wishes to take to Virginia," replied Mrs. Carleton.

"We will all join her there," said the Colonel, "and then we can walk back along the shore to our boat."

On arriving at the long ledge of rocks that ran straight out into the ocean, and which they called the " Whale's Back," they entered the little cove that was situated on the side nearest to the castle. There was Miss Vyvyan's basket half filled with the shells that Cora so much desired ; but where was she ?

In another moment, Cora with her quick step was springing up to the highest part of the rocks. A shriek of anguish from the child, and the cry in her former baby language, " Anna be back, Anna be back," brought her parents instantly to her side. Looking from the high wall that nature had formed, and across the larger cove on the other side, they saw far out toward the open sea Miss Vyvyan's upturned face. She was floating on an enormous wave which was bearing her rapidly toward the shore.

" Oh Anna, poor Anna; save her Dudley," cried Mrs. Carleton, believing anything possible to the brave and kind-hearted man, who had dared and surmounted all obstacles for her own sake.

" Yes, dearest ; yes, trust me. I will do my utmost," replied the Colonel, quickly scaling the outer side of the cliff, and dashing over and among the broken masses of rock that laid between him and the sea. Throwing off his hat and heavy uniform coat, he stood with extended arms at the water's edge, exactly at the spot where he knew he wave would strike. Miss Vyvyan was being swiftly borne toward him and was within a few feet distance.

"Keep calm," he called to her, "for heaven's
sake, keep calm, and I can save you."

The great wave bearing its living burden, broke
upon the beach with unusual violence. Colonel
Carleton was struck and thrown far up toward the
shore by its mighty force. In another instant, he
was on his feet again, rushing forward àfter the re-
ceding water, which was carrying Miss Vyvyan
out. She still floated on the crest of the wave.
Raising one hand and unclasping it, she threw
upon the beach a small white shell, saying as she
did so, "for dear Cora." She saw the friendly out-
stretched arm of the brave man ; she looked up to
the rocks ; she saw the pure, classic features of
gentle, loving Ada, paralyzed with distress, white
as marble, pallid and death-like, as on the day that
she had kissed them back to life seven years before. She saw the beautiful child, who was so
precious to her ; she noted the terror, pain and
love in its fair, young face. She heard the sweet
voice calling "Anna be back." She saw no more,
the waters covered her ; the same ocean which
had brought her to the island, claimed her for its
own and bore her away forever.

. . ..

Many summers and winters have come and gone,
and long years have passed away since the ladies
and their dear little one lived on the island. The
flowers have faded and the trees of the forest have
died with time, but neither time nor death has
power to kill the love of a true heart ; that lives
on forever and ever and, phœnix-like, exists on its